**BOOKS BY HOUSE OF NEHESI PUBLISHERS**

The Salt Reaper
Poems from the flats
*Lasana M. Sekou*

Friendly Anger
The Rise of The Labor Movement in St. Martin
*Joseph H. Lake, Jr.*

Salted Tongues
Modern Literature in St. Martin
*Fabian Adekunle Badejo*

Somebody Blew Up America & Other Poems
*Amiri Baraka*

The Essence of Reparations
*Amiri Baraka*

1963 - A Landmark Year in St. Martin
A Retrospective Look
*Daniella Jeffry-Pilot*

The House That Jack Built and Other Plays
*Louie Laveist*

Same Sea ... Another Wave
*Cynthia Wilson*

Words Need Love Too
*Kamau Brathwaite*

Coming, Coming Home - Conversations II
Western Education & The Caribbean Intellectual
*George Lamming*

Regreso, regreso al hogar - Conversaciones II
La educación occidental y el intelectual Caribeño
*George Lamming*

Songs & Images of St. Martin
*Charles Borromeo Hodge*

Brotherhood of The Spurs
(fiction, short stories)
*Lasana M. Sekou*

# The Angel Horn

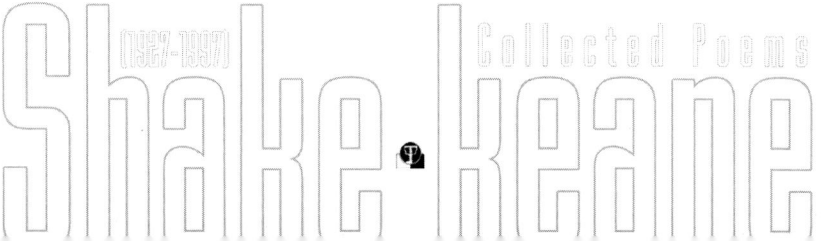

(1927-1997) Collected Poems
Shake Keane

HOUSE OF NEHESI PUBLISHERS
P.O. Box 460
Philipsburg, St. Martin
Caribbean

WWW.HOUSEOFNEHESIPUBLISH.COM

© 2005 by Margaret Bynoe.
All rights reserved.
ISBN: 0-913441-66-X
LC Control Number: 2004110155

All rights to these poems, including performance rights, are reserved.
No part of this book may be reproduced, stored in or introduced into a retrieval system, or transmitted in any form or by any means, electronic or mechanical, including photocopying, recording, or by any information source and retrieval system, without permission in writing from the copyright owner and Publisher.

Acknowledgments: Lamming, George. Letter. 8 Dec. 2003. Lamming, George. Letter. 2 Jan. 2004; Dr. Margaret Bynoe.

Sources consulted for "About the Author" (pp. 184-185 of this book): Margaret Bynoe. George Lamming. Nanton, Philip. "In Memoriam - Ellsworth McGranahan 'Shake' Keane, 1927-1997," *Wasafiri* Spring 1998: 40+. Nanton, Philip. "Real Keane," *Caribbean Beat* Mar.-Apr. 2004. Nanton, Philip. "Shake Keane's Poetic Legacy," The Society For Caribbean Studies Annual Conference Papers. Ed. by Sandra Courtman. 2000: 1. Rohlehr, Gordon. "The Problem of the Problem of Form," *The Shape of That Hurt and Other Essays*. Port of Spain: Longman, 1992: 28. Val, Wilmer. "Shake Keane - The anger behind a free form of jazz" (Obituaries), *The Guardian* 13 Nov. 1997: 18. A version of "Mistress Mucket's Funeral" (pg. 29) was published as "Shaker Funeral" in *L'oubli - Poems by E. McG. Keane* (1950). The "dedication" of Book Two (pg. 39) appeared as a poem by the same name in *L'oubli - Poems by E. McG. Keane* (1950). A version of "Nancitori" (pg. 127) was presented, with changes, as "Nancitori With Drums" at the Lyric Theatre (N.D.).

Cover and graphics design by Sundiata Lake, S.L DesignMedia
Cover art: "S Keane" 2004, charcoal by Joe Dominique
Photography: Courtesy Margaret Bynoe

*To Allan, Julian, Roland.*

# CONTENTS

*page*

| | |
|---|---|
| **BOOK ONE - SMILES IN THE HEART OF THE FAMILY** | 1 |
| Roundtrip | 3 |
| Private Prayer | 15 |
| Hide and Seek | 16 |
| Girls and Boys | 18 |
| Unu Coonoomoonoo | 19 |
| Nallidge | 21 |
| Apartite | 22 |
| Hammosapiens | 23 |
| Me'N Angie | 24 |
| School for Two Voices | 27 |
| Mistress Mucket's Funeral | 29 |
| Public Prayer | 33 |
| People Like We | 36 |
| **BOOK TWO - EVE AND ADAMS** | 39 |
| Of Love and Rivers | 41 |
| Love Story (2) | 42 |
| My Love My Hot Eyes | 43 |
| Three Roofs in Roseau | 44 |
| Narcissus Descending | 46 |
| Coming Back | 47 |
| Boy with Tail | 50 |
| Finding | 51 |
| Dustbin Lids | 52 |
| First Live with Guitar | 53 |
| I Pronounce You | 54 |
| Barrouallie Dawn | 55 |
| Adeyemi | 60 |
| Love Story (13) | 62 |

| | |
|---|---|
| Peanuts -- 1946 | 63 |
| Love Story (1) | 66 |
| One Woman | 67 |
| Love Story (3) | 68 |
| Nothing Ventured | 69 |
| Love Story (21) | 71 |
| Lost and Found Lost | 73 |

## BOOK THREE - THIRTEEN STUDIES IN HOME ECONOMICS — 77

| | |
|---|---|
| (Lesson One: Family Figgers) | 79 |
| (Lesson Two: Options) | 80 |
| (Lesson Three: Papa Amoeba) | 81 |
| (Lesson Four: Maturity) | 83 |
| (Lesson Five: Per Capita Per Annum) | 84 |
| (Lesson Six: How to Count) | 88 |
| (Lesson Seven: Credential) | 89 |
| (Lesson Eight: Here Am I Send Me) | 92 |
| (Lesson Nine: Underwater Games) | 94 |
| (Lesson Ten: Man About the House) | 96 |
| (Lesson Eleven: Who's Yo Father) | 99 |
| (Lesson Twelve: My Neighbour Plum Tree) | 100 |
| (Lesson Thirteen: Song of the Underdeveloped Casino) | 104 |

## BOOK FOUR - PALM AND OCTOPUS — 109

| | |
|---|---|
| Bananas | 111 |
| Dance for Me | 113 |
| Rise Up Within Me | 114 |
| Two Years Ago | 115 |
| There Was Not | 116 |
| In This Ancient Bay | 117 |
| Singing This Morning | 118 |
| And Will You | 119 |
| You Will Remember | 120 |
| Palm and Octopus | 121 |

| | |
|---|---:|
| Frogs | 122 |
| I Need To Apologize | 123 |
| **BOOK FIVE - THE WISDOM-KEEPERS** | **125** |
| Nancitori | 127 |
| Kaiso Kaiso | 135 |
| Jumbie | 143 |
| **BOOK SIX - BROOKLYN THEMES** | **163** |
| Nostrand Avenue | 165 |
| Juke Box | 166 |
| Ruth | 167 |
| Gwen Sings | 168 |
| Sonnet for Margaret | 169 |
| J. Sligh: A Parable | 170 |
| Love in Bed/stuy -- Brooklyn | 172 |
| The Bar | 174 |
| The Islands (A Toast) | 178 |
| **EPILOGUE** | **179** |
| Angel Horn | 181 |
| ABOUT THE AUTHOR | 183 |

*The Angel Horn* is vintage Shake Keane. This collection of poems spanning a period of 40 years reveals the best of Keane, his mastery of the folk culture, play on words, use of nation language and of musical symbols and themes, and the integration of rhymes and riddles into his work. His "nonsense" talk and satirical mien expose a kind of irreverence as the author pokes fun at the society and life, recapturing his early life in London, his frustration on his return home *(St. Vincent)* and his self-imposed exile in New York. Keane is a poet about which more needed to be known and this collection will go a far way in doing so. Admirers and friends have long awaited this collection and will certainly not be disappointed.

- Adrian Fraser, PhD.
*University of The West Indies*
St. Vincent and The Grenadines

BOOK ONE

# SMILES IN THE HEART OF THE FAMILY

## ROUNDTRIP

AROUND 1950
in London
you could count the Vincentians
on the fingers of one hand --
I mean
we really uses to do that --
sitting down in a pub somewhere
wearing gloves
all five of us would hold up a finger each
and drink to Sin-Vincent --
beer -- out of a big glass --
later we called it a mug --
Our fingers were different-coloured
especially without gloves

The youngest amongst us was learning Norwegian
with this chick from Norway
He was hoping to end up
Ambassador in Oslo
to the London St. Vincentians
He drank beer the most

The Oldest would weep from time to time
for home
He is a Carib from Owia named Nero

(That same year there was a bad fog
it started a Monday and got better and better
till by Friday you couldn't see
if it was your own English girlfriend

feeling your hand by the bus stop)

In those days the Caribs didn't come into it much

The Chinese
either said what Confucius said
or gnawed at their own chow mein
in restaurants on Gerrard Street
all fitted with dragonic lanterns
and fat-bellied statues
with beards growing
not on but underneath their chins

Spanish people
used to come to London every year
and tap-dance

Indians-and-so
Well they were all back in St. Vincent
with good hair
nice tenor voices
no music
and names from Scotland

Africans were beardless
but they studied accountancy
whereas they should have been doing law
They wore good suits
but had bad hair
and long-tooth wooden combs
instead of combs
They knew where there were drums
if you asked them
also drank beer

and were black

One of them said
He knew a place where we could get some history

The moment the five of us left **The Pub**
the Westindies came to London
People from Jamaica
and Trinidad
and even Anguilla
joined the family all of a sudden
We held up a lot of fingers
later drank a lot of beer
laughed at the natives
simply because we knew
how to pronounce Grenada
and they didn't

It's true that one Jamaican
asked me what part of Jamaica
St. Vincent was in
He lived in 24 A Basset Rd.
Ladbroke Grove London W.12
(His special pleasure
was farting loud on the underground train)

And somebody asked
when the Martiniquans
and the Surinamese
were going to come over
But apart from that
everything went fine

And when the time came

we let the Africans into the secrets
of the Calypso
I borrowed one of their combs

But wait a minute
there was a Spanish chap
from Panama
used to sing in a night-club in West Kensington
-- just like Nat King Cole --
No sooner did he settle in to life in The Pub
than he began to boast
that he was going around proclaiming his independence
in all the public toilets in the district

The Norwegian and me
check some of the toilets
We found a lot of yellow posters marked
Long Live Santa Maria

And hello
Something else did go wrong one day
when we met a Chinese fellow from Jamaica
name of Pastor Sutherland
The African chap who lent me the comb
said he know a guy from Pakistan
whose name was Creighton
Pakistan? We asked, Pakistan?
Then again for instance
one day a Black Carib guy from Belize
walked into the family pub
and held up his finger
Doku the African said this guy was an Amerindian

(after inspecting the finger)
and an Indian chappie from Mauritius
named Dupont
said it was true
His French girlfriend said she had heard
there was a Carib stone
in the Carnegie Public Library in K/town St. Vincent

But apart from that . . .

AROUND 1959
a fellow from Ghana
by the name of Ananse Abrahams
turned up in London
and right away started buying up old houses
in Brixton
He is a very hard man to rent from
but most of us had to turn to him in the end
because the English landladies claimed
their neighbours didn't like them renting us rooms

The Jamaican Chinese fellow
started to take his girlfriend to restaurants
in Gerrard Street

Our Youngest thought of calling himself ex

By 1964 this Ananse fellow
owned a whole pub in Brixton
The family was getting bigger and bigger

A Bermudan feller
who had lived in America
showed us a poster of Che Guevara

He the person showing us the poster
had a limp in his left shoulder
and a scar
where a white cop in Detroit
had banged him with a blackjack
He said James Baldwin himself
had also examined that scar
James Baldwin? we asked, -- Oh, James **Ballwin**
Yes he said

We had long ago stopped calling ourselves Vincentians
because the family name had changed to Westindian

And if it wasn't for that blow on the left shoulder
we might still have been calling ourselves that

But the night after the scar
the Trinidadian said his Swiss wife
woke up screaming
saying she had had a dream
in which her husband looked like Pandit Nehru
Nkrumah Angela Davis Mau tse Che
Julius Nyereretung a Hungarian peasant
and the Mighty Sparrow
all at the same time
and all of them had black fingers

A lot of the younger heads
said they were having a similar dream
but without the Hungarian peasant
The Ananse fellow said he dreamed one day
that he was living forever
He said he was surprised when he woke up

to found himself alive

Shortly after that he sold the pub
and opened a business in St. Vincent
re-treading motor-car tires
He said he know the place well
because he had lived there before long ago

By instinct we started to call ourselves
Sisters and brothers
(But nobody can say peace and love sweet like a Jamaican)

THEN

One day the African chap ran into The Pub
bleeding from a riot in Nottinghill Gate
We gave him a mug of beer to calm him down
And the English chap who now owned the pub
sent out to Brixton market
for some yam zabocca and saltfish
so that the poor fellow could at least
cook himself a decent meal
when he returned to de damn Gate

After this African chap had calmed down a bit
we asked him if he still knew
where we could get the drums
He said he would have to go home for them
We begged him while he home
to see if he could find us the history too

That night the five of us Vincentians
decide to take some of the history
and the drums

and go back home

To mark the occasion
we all take off we gloves and throw them way
We travel most of the way by Pan-American jet
The year was Christmas 1970

FIRST thing when we hit St. Vincent
we notice
is
everybody have good hair
(Oh I forget to tell you all the time
one of us white)

Well we not settlin een **so** well
But we smiles a lot when we think about the family

We meet every Sunday morning in this year
People calls it a pub
maybe because we drinks beer here
out of a bottle
and is only Reggae records we plays
Dutch beer is not so good though
so most time we imbibes our own local overproof
local

And we settles down to some good old limetalk
(For an instant
we does still laugh bout this Bermuda feller
what he tell us
bout how when he first see snow in New York
how he run outside and bring back a handful
put it in the frying pan and fry it
just so

and mind you --
that was **before** he get the blow on his left shoulder)

But we not settlin een so well

We thinks a lot about the family
and all them days we may be waste
when we used to hold up we finger
and argue
whether if yam eat sweeter in Europe
or in St. Vincent

The family is mostly all home now

The oldest of us is not resting so good at nights
Sometime he cries
(A Indian doctor is treating him
He has a real name from India
But he don't use souse)

On top of all that
Nero grandson just left grammar school
sudden so
after five years
say he can't understand all this rollox they telling he
bout Carl Marks Anthony
   -- and he don't even like football --
Before he gone crazy and start to breed woman
a politician feller get him a job
in the Tax Office

The other day he Nero was pacing some strong
outside the gate by Arnos Vale Cricket Ground
A o-lady name Tantie Merle

decide to tell he where Pakistan is
He nearly kill she
Bangla-Desh is another thing

We also reads a lot
The other day we find a book
by Earl Kirby our local archangelist
with all the carib stones in it
The youngest one of us can draw and read the best
He can draw carib stones quite nicely
He also keep the drums and the history safe
He say it is his duty
and we trust him

Not couple months back
we resume contact with this Ananse fellow
He said his Vincentian wife always tellin him
to change his way a little
and think about the future
And too -- besides --
too much stone-headed people blockin his road
So he sell out the motor-car-tyre business
and open a church

His new business makes him travel all about
And being he is constant giving us news
about other mentions in the family home
we are definitely back in correspondence
through this Ananse fellow

The Jamaicachynee chap frinstance
wrote us to say
that after considerable roundsing around

he lately also form a **Union** of his own
He now writin a bible
title
Solid Rock Underneath The Archipelago
S R U T A for short

But to date is the youngest one of we
doing the most correspondence
**He** doing a correspondence course
in **community development**
And he lately write Hong Kong for the external exam
in yoga and Karachi

Couple weeks back he changes he name to Doku Jamal
and he also corresponding with a young lady
in Venezuela
name Maria Amalivaca y Pedros
(we don't know yet what the why stand for)
The Carib guy from Belize
write say she must be have Amerindian blood
(by the way
he now living in Honduras
and he have a steelband using trapset
and a pair of Indian table drums)

AMALIVACA now
Like she starting to have married on she mind
She say she thinking of coming over
and start a dancin-school in the yard
Our youngest not clear
how he feel bout that
but he can really smile-dance dem Reggae records

rooty smile

Nero claim everything does have to dance
when it hear certain sounds
Even last Sunday in the middle of he overproof
our Oldest put down one bawlin
seh wha de hell he five finger
only smilin smilin so for

Yesterday
He Nero
and Doku
just lef cool so go buy a new book
name Teach Yourself Spanish

(St. Vincent, March 1975 - February 1977)

**PRIVATE PRAYER**

*(for Walter Rodney)*

To understand
How the whole thing run
I have to ask my parents
And even my daughter and son

To understand the form
Of compromise I am
I must in my own voice ask
How the whole thing run

To ask
Why I don't dream
In the same language I live in
I must rise up
Among syllables of my parents
In the land which I am
And form
A whole daughter a whole son
Out of the compromise
Which I am

To understand history
I have to come home

(London, 24 April 1973)

## HIDE AND SEEK

*(for Jessica's daughter, Accabre)*

**MY papa**
**Your papa**
**Live across the sea**
**Every night**
**They have a quarrel**
**This is what they say**

Chatoyer
Where yo dey

Quako Babu
Where yo day

INK STINK PEPPERMINT
SURE TO SMELL ABOMINABLE STINK

Open Juba cubbitch
Open brother Belele
The family deh in deh

**Di mamma di mamma**
**Bore booti la**
**Cochon ha-papa large ha**

Children children
Yes papa
Where yo bin to
Far across the sea, papa
      Hittyhopia where yo day
Chatoyer say
Tomorrow night

When the moon out-off
Come down
Down together in the dark
Spread out you hand
Like yo know is who
You are
And the catcher will know
What to do

AKRA BAKRA
MOONLIGHT TOUCH HER
OUT GOES YOU

Now all-you wash you face-and hand
And to sleep you go
Leave the sea to me

Short little while
Wake up clean-foot and smile
In the heart of the family

**One two three**
**I catch yo**

(London, 20 April 1973)

## GIRLS AND BOYS
*(for Maidowa)*

GIRLS have three hands
Boys have two
Girls hold things in their mouth
If their other two hands occupied
Boys rest them on the ground

Girls like to frighten boys
If they taller than them
Boys frighten mules in the park
'Cause mules are taller than girls
We all are afraid of the dark

Boys care each other
Girls groom each other
Hands are for sweetness and pride

Girls like windy weather in their veins
Boys fight the weather
They both like, though

When boys in trouble
They stand up and stagger
When girls in trouble
They lie down
Consider

Boys love girls
And to be free like the weather
Girls are the weather
And they love boys

(London, 20 April 1973)

## UNU COONOOMOONOO

                        I KNOW yo in dey

                        Mek yo don t come

out and talk

. . . yo **l i a r** yo

    e bawl out
from de place e was hidin inna

           if you name

                        man

        buwait nuh
    cha bwoy

           j e s u wept

                    hot forra dammer and so on

        is big dis bwoy get big so

        big stick

        full belly big brains

    but look pon me days nuh

cha

    *conio su madre* an' so on

                            evenself if

(who say so)
    is me an dem bwoy
not a red cent

        but de women an dem

        an de young people dem

**cheeseanrice**

              and so on . . .

    Is me alone tomek up me face den

           and soon . . .

    And soon

        Just

as

        he talkin so

so on

        and

so

        fort

e

come

**outta** de place

    e was alltime hidin inna

                (Cologne, June 1970)

## NALLIDGE
*(for Mark Williams)*

Brown people not brown you know
I mix wid one-o-dem last night

Yellow people don't really all yellow
Is only dey eyes mek dem look so

Red people is now nearly all dead people

White people try

              and can't bite
Not evenself when yo live inside o' dey mout'

Black people black you hear
One-o-dem promise me something

Tonight

           Dat is why

G r e e n  p e o p l e

            does come up to me

                      and

                            ask me

                                      hello

Every night

                                        (London, 13 April 1973)

## APARTITE

ARWE binna call ye
                buwen we call yo  yo didn hear
                        an if yo hear yo didn look
                                an if yo look yo didn see
                                          an if yo see

yo didn blow win pon cotton gie we fo smell

                                                              (Cologne, June 1970)

## HAMMOSAPIENS

AH tell yo ah sick

                        yo tell me ah have rittum

Ah tell yo ah want free

                        yo tell me ah happy areddy

So ah get critical
Ah tell yo ah pritty

                        yo tell me
                        such and such is pritty

Listen to Me

                        Yo tell me yo have to fine out
                        if I have a histry
                        furss

ah tell yo haul yo arse

                        Yo tell me dat isn't biblical

Well if yo know so much bout so much
how come
yo so darn wrong bout me

                                              (Cologne, May 1969)

## ME'N ANGIE
*(for Angela Davis)*

IS de love-and-brimmin lady
and de rain come down
              so long so long
is foot no road river no boat
is fire brimmin over
wid tears and a fire
        bun so long so long
and is allfire who wears
        afrika like a crown on me head
              and a lump in me throat
name dead name dead
        ANGIE I have dis pain inna hereso
so long
        so long de rain come down
        though the sun like a crowbar diggin out
me eye
        and I wish to know
so I wish to know    so long I wish to know
yo name . . .
        Jumbie people walkin in me head
 talkin all over nothin
white as snow
        and I is a clown swingin low
so long
so long I wish to know yo name

IS bloodblues brudder soledad

        mamma alabama

        is a gun-slum city breakin out

        over cane over corn

and sometime down here

when cousin sun bite out de sky

        ignite me eye in island over island

        I does cry

black river brown hair hammer and stammer

alone wid song

bawlin down roadriver

        for all me angelas dead and born

        so long betray

        so

        long

betray

    so

    long

           ANGIE
           I HAS dis PAIN inna hereso
       and
    dis
CHAIN

           of island I wear so long

Jumbie-rain
are talkin

in my nose
and in
my
head

sunlight w a l k i n g

                        me back over

       riverboat

       rocksong

     like me'n Angie coming
      for all those
           damage and done
                by sun and sea
                and
                done
                love
                   by me

'cause
I
Name
    Judas
Ignition
    Asanthane
Crowbar
    Sometimeish

Black

                                        (Cologne, 13 July 1972)

## SCHOOL FOR TWO VOICES

A TRUE little island in a deep blue sea
**a true likkle island in a deep blue sea**
A sound little mind in a sound body
**a sung likkle island in a sung body**

                        **Yes teacher**

Now children
An island is a portion of land
Entirely surround by sea and sand
            **Dear teacher**
Speak the truth and speak it over
            **Dorg-dung is a compung nung**
Carry your load and falter never
            **With a stinkin scent**
            **As to knock you dung**

Please children

Likkle Red Robin Hood
            **Please teacher**
Is good dear children good
            **Dolphus feelin up Gwen**

Is good      good
            **She eyes like-a come-back-again**

O you sinners of Class II iniquity
Pay up yor sin tax with alacrity
Or you will never reach God's University

            **Come on teacher**
            **Constance   open   Nennen   coop**

Monkey mudder were boilin soup
> **Eat all-a nennen chicken soup**

Money stood up and leggo poop

Ah children    children
> **Poor teacher**

John Jookum de Lasselas of Genoa

RICH MAN POOR MAN FOREMAN TIEF
WHITE MAN BLACK MAN BEGGARMAN CHIEF
> He done fought in the battle of Tea

> Dear children    dear dear children

AN ISLAND IS A PORTION OR PIECE OF SAN'

ENTIRELY MOUNTED BY WOMAN AN' MAN

> Yes children    yes

**Yes**

(Cologne, 28 July 1972)

## MISTRESS MUCKET'S FUNERAL

SORROW sin-
bound, pelting din
big chorusclash
o' the mourners;
eyes red
with a shout for the dead,
yelling crash-
ing sadness in
the dusty tread
o' the mourners.

> **Sweet Mother gone**
> **to the by and by,**
> **follow her to the brink o' Zion.**

Wave wave
as they roared to the grave
a drench-song
soul-thunder
was **aymens** through
the wind, shrieks, flews,
and eyes were strong,
for 'twas madness gave
them dirge, that grew
made thunder.

Drums, flags,
pious rags
O' robes stenching
wheat;

mitre o' tattered straw
bamboo crozier
wagged by wind's clenching
deathwind that bragged
sorrow, smattered
o' sweat.

Saints in blue
bathrobes flew
about the ranks
o' the sinners,
and froth-lipped virgins
with powdered skins
and frocks that stank
with the slime and the stew
from the purged away sins
o' the sinners;

And heads were white
in starched cloth . . . Bright
was the blood from the eyes
o' the candles;
and the "horn of the Ram
of the great I AM"
spoke hoarse in cries;
and crowned with the light
o' the Judah Lamb
were the candles.

> **Lord delivered Daniel**
> **from shame's mouth.**
> **(o strong, o strong roll Jordan.)**

> **Lord deliver our Mother**
> **gone to the Glory Hope.**
> **gone to the Glory Home, gone to Zion.**

All God's brothers
were loud, and the ten
holy lampers were
reeking in smoke;
and the "valley of sod-
and-shadow," Staff-Rod,
was blenched as the cankering
sweat o' men
and the reeking o' God
in the smoke.

> **His willing be,**
> **Mother gone,**
> **Jordan deep,**
> **her soul is strong,**
> **Follow her to the brink o' Zion.**

And now the grave
was washed in a wave
o' wails and a
city o' stars
that dribbled and burned
in the tears that turned
hot sins, on the smoke-white pillars . . .
But their sorrow was yells,
and their faith was brave,
as the blood-blemished lambs
piled big on the grave

their city o' wax and stars.

>   Sweet Mother gone,
>   Queen o' Mansions-over-Jordan.
>   O strong . . .
>   Leave her safe on the brink o' Zion.

(St. Vincent, April 1950)

## PUBLIC PRAYER

*(for my daughter Sareth, if ever she is born)*

CHILDREN-OH
>    take this cup
>       upon my knee
>       Sup where

**Amen**

>    yo see  me
>    bloody kneelin
>          burnin here
>    in this pitch road
>    Quench the heat
Children

**Amen**

>    All-yo thinks
>     yo see
>    wickedness

**Amen**

>    Is me
>      and this
>    backwardness
>    inna me

>    Bite the rain
>    Children-Oh

>>       Pitch the road
>>       wid pitch
>>       Walk rightfully
>>       thereupon

**Amen**

    Mother Sareth
    think on she
before thy cup break
    and the road empty

**Amen**

    Fight
    the heat
    of the sinner-man

**Amen**

    Who sell yo blood
    to the Egyptolite
Who mouth betray
    the Shepherd
    and the mother
        Who pitch the road
    backwards
    unto weariness . . .

**Amen**

Jesus
    unclean Jesus
help me children to
    CHILDREN is FEELINS
feelin
    for a chinks
in thy garment
    of darkness
waitin
    for the veil
    of the temple
to rent

                                                            **Amen**

     If all-yo
know
     taste
and see He bloodlight breakin

        Shed me
           shed me

                                          **Amen**

        Pitch yo road
        with gladness
        make haste
and feed ye
        thereupon

                      But verily verily remember me
                  The very waters
                          of wickedness yea and love

        floweth
        from my knee

'cause I name
Judas
Ignition
Asanthane
Crowbar
Sometimeish

Black

                                          **Amen**

                              (London, 24 April 1973)

## PEOPLE LIKE WE

MAKONAIMA say
                           touch me finger
                           and let today
                           be the day
                           when all mountain
                           lock the finger
                           in the midst of the sea

Qualeva say

    Yes

Wind say

                           touch me throat
                           and let today
                           be the day
                           to thread all voice
                           through all valley
                           and let there be
                           in the midst of all music
                           one note

Drum say

    yes

Flute rattle and sitar

stand up like lip

            and breast

            and finger

        making

one mountain

        dreaming

one star

        locking

one love

        in the midst of the sea

People like we say

        yes

*(Produced at the closing session of CARIFESTA,*
*Guyana, September 1972)*

BOOK TWO

# EVE AND ADAMS
## LOVE, MATING, AND GOD-MOTHER POEMS

1946-1979

*TO...*
*... SHYLY a little,*
*because your innocence is still*
*innocent of itself,*
*and you have not*
*learned your modesty by heart,*
*my thoughts' embraces*
*of your soul*
*and every searching their sadness*

*but since*
*sighs are not fulfilled*
*in their own due longing,*
*and hope remains mercy*
*only until the warm*
*love of its deception*
*waltzes over the edge of*
*our one lost moment,*

*my searching is forever . . .*
*and so be your innocence.*

*(St. Vincent, 1946)*

## OF LOVE AND RIVERS

My love are you strong
I will bring my life to you
Like a bundle of washing
And all they say is my soul
Will bring
Like washing to your sweet rivers
    And will you say this
    Will you say
        Drink deep
        Sink deep
        Dream deeply of cleansing
And of rivers

My love are you strong
I will bring my sins to you
On the breast of your rivers
Will cling
Will pray we like washing
Be washed alone and away
    And will you say this
    Will you say
        Sigh sweet
        Die gentle
        Dream deeply of cleansing
In our love-like rivers

(St. Vincent, 1973. Remade from an earlier poem)

## LOVE STORY (2)

We looked at the moon together,
Big and wise there.
We look at our hearts together
Fussed in our eyes there
Love-pools.

The moon is an eye upon all things.
Love is strong beyond all things,

Beyond the life, the death-life,
The biogenesis of all things.

Now I look at the moonless night
Wondering if somewhere beyond
This old meaningless night
Is an eye upon all shattered eyes.

For love and life and the moon can be broken
          beyond all things

(St. Vincent, 1950)

## MY LOVE MY HOT EYES

My love my hot eyes
Dawning over your breasts
Retrieve no warning sighs
Rise
Where no mirrorness
Of pooled regrets rise

My love my hot eyes dawning
Light me ways into the full blooded flash
Surprise no prodigal wish
Wise in the dark returning

Oh my love my hot eyes

(St. Vincent, 1952)

## THREE ROOFS IN ROSEAU

There are three roofs left now in Roseau
after the hurricane

Zitrea and her two daughters
were found
drowned there

Cities are made
of things destroyed
and things created

and a capital city was Roseau

Surrounded
by large loud wind
Dominica became
our lost special island
our Lord's
of three roofs
and of silence

Roseau
a slim reed of memory
left so now
left so

Disaster like love
like memory
is always understated

Like Zitrea
whom I loved
many days upon a Lord's day

many years
before the hurricane indeed

My dear lost and dated Zitrea
Though I have nothing now
I will not be silent

There are three roofs still standing in Roseau

(St. Vincent, 31 August 1979)

## NARCISSUS DESCENDING

RAGING as rain on sensual pools
I come
fonding nothing but my fresh fondled passion
and a fool's rippling eye for flesh

Wearing my own narrative
like the spruce lyric of lithe white walls
or arrogantly ageing with the candlelight
I come drinking to you my lovelimpid one

Hounding desire through the tail cool smoke
forested in froth and fire
find you

Bludgeoned afresh
baffled and sparsely wounded
flourish you
my flaming dread one my ecstasy of shame

(London, 13 July 1963)

## COMING BACK

BEACHES are full of old nails after rain
a shivering heat in my belly
like love
like disasterlike
old words I found once on a rusty tin in January
as a child speeding past my first temptation
don't go out go out either in the hot sun nor
in the pouring rain
pride like the sea secretes little by little
odd kinds of music
you might get old nails in your little foot

Come in don't come in
the house of the Lord without a good hat not on --
the whole congregation sitting up like little children

That time was the magic before he
hadn't exactly risen like glory over the nest
where she would die
then all the cornets and the small drums
would yell in my belly something like power
would he really come one day
to make a sentence
        containing any or all of the following
all old nails on a beach
think of all the music you might lose
                    just constructing sentences

People said so she said
everything seems easier when you learn the words

as I fled like disaster past my first temptation
the teacher and the preacher not caring
or not needing to go out
in the dirty rain said
he would later have big trouble with a mustard seed

Old words and new coins in my rusty tin
dancing on one good foot looking
over the other shoulder
I felt I couldn't hold her but she
took me up from out of all of that wet wet tide
and loved me like I was a man
but how could she
      where drums and cornets and church choirs
replaced all music
all her power
how could she take me out to pasture

So she laughing quite louder than she could pray
circular within that certain reality of sand
encircled
by havens the shape of wind
ships and wind and spray
castles of spray
and ships the nominees of our joint disaster --

she sent me away to love her

Though it was moonlight the rain purred
like beasts all through the August nights

That year much later
clusters of shining in wet sand
she secretly waited

    should I come surging back old nails
and pride shivering in my belly it really feels
a little like power something like love

(Cologne and Georgetown, Guyana, February 1970)

## BOY WITH TAIL

If this was home
I'd be runnin a little thing with her
Enjoyin the fuckin nonsense

Knowin that if I failed
All my friends
And all my family

And all my home would say

Come back again
If you can't win
Lose

But if this was home
I would have to choose
Between responsibility and experience

And I would have to fail

(Koln, December 1970)

## FINDING

THEY needn't have asked the way
But they did
And the girl found a new season
And the boy found another sky
Where the juices came early
Falling over them like spring

They needn't have taken that way
But the boy and the girl
Trembled to find when they did
That they could lose each other
Under the same sky
Going the same way
In the same season

So they died
Telling each other secrets they already knew

(Koln, June 1971)

## DUSTBIN LIDS

We were just foolin
dangerous kids
Esther by the school window
played with her left ear
wantin to tell me a secret
dangerous gesture
We played with rocks
and atones a game of shields
of dustbin lids clever I declare
I still have a mark just below
the belt
deft there but too damn slow
with my dustbin shield
THAT yielded a kiss from her
my first

I have never
recovered from her secrets

(Koln, 26 July 1972)

## FIRST LIVE WITH GUITAR

                           ALL day
                         she would speak
                   of shrouds
                   and wings

                play
             with small treasures
           a dove's beak
         a knitted star
     a guitar with yellow strings

  he wrote of this
all day long

                     she
             noting no change in him
           would say
         nothing
      but dreamt his name
   sang once of yellow clouds
a raven's kiss

at night

he came

and put away
her childish things

                                                      (Koln, 6 August 1972)

## I PRONOUNCE YOU

WHAT words, if she were lost, or near,
would re-assemble her?

What proof what cost what wound
would make my fear
resemble her?

The joints of all our years are intricate
and aloof.

(Koln, 21 November 1972)

## BARROUALLIE DAWN

(NOT yet.
Two hours, then the sweat . . . )

Mornings when the sea hungers and is hollow
And over the hollow sea
the mountain greenbrained
an ancient nippled head
roars as if to settle
sinks
like all death to the sea-bed
               which is the dawn of the sea
muddling blood and yellow and hollow

Time enough for a quick wisdom
A half-truth half-exploding in the larynx

Noises from her thatched head
Trickling up and down
The canyons of our pillow

(You can close your book of dreams now
You can close your book of dreams now
Now the sweet . . . )

MANGO season
fruit-fights delight in doorways of mud and wattle
Soon a talon of flies
will make the air unfeasible

Wet-sanded girls with their tender crooked glances
The young men muscled like Christ or cattle
half-naked seriously unemployed by the sea

not even pounding almonds
down below the wharf
in between sessions of harpoon practice
And little Violet Quow
will have to have her corner-mouth rubbed
with Canadian Healing Oil

And seeing that it always drizzles here
after nights of hips and happenstances
soon the drizzle will wonder
why suddenly Sareth is afraid

SOON the early ants will be hauling pick and shovel
over the gravel that finds the mountain

Bolts will fall away from the doors
of three shops

An ass will stand up
and count the fleas under his arm

Next door the cow will glare at the bucket
and prepare for all that all over again

The bus will blow

Already children are returning
over the mud-sided valley over Glebe Hill
with their bundles of bush

If this is perhaps reality
why does it have
to come hiccuping out of nowhere
rum yellowing its knees its breath
sixpence in its pocket

imagined essences in its head

Last night we said that virtue comes out
of the morning, and the stale steam that curls
off at dawn from the hot damp thatch on my
friend's hovel might perhaps be significant
beyond anything in our knowledge. Emanations.
Essences. And yet in the same breath we
drawled that awareness was the only crime,
that the soul bombarded by impressions of

beauty and horror should not give in to the
circumscription of its own ability to be impressed
by beauty and horror, but should assume a focal
point where beauty and horror converge into
something of which it cannot possibly become
fully aware -- Africa? -- God? -- (We, like almost
everyone this year, had been drinking of course).
Something SOME thing who is beauty and horror is
Located always one intuition beyond our awareness;
and ITS religion is sustained only by the perpetual
will be be defeated. All this I told her to understand.

To be converted is to sustain your first
defeat, -- the one that was not your doing;
to be pious is to encourage many more defeats
by setting your will always on the unattainable.
For piety is not in the multitude of
spiritual things we have conquered, but in the
enslavement to whatever thing will not cease
from conquering us, -- to almost find your
roots, your original myth, and at the same

time your highest achievement but one.
Now at dawn all this is trash, or merely true.

Facts, Numbers, and the Sweat. At dawn
God changes shoes with "Reality." But there
is much reality in a bottle. Here on earth
and away from Africa the unattainable still
holds highest value; You are successful not
merely because you are but because you try;
you are more honorably satisfied when you try
to be than when you are. Our teacher always
said so. Last night it seemed that to be
liberated is to find your roots and to
experience the joy of being vanquished by it.
like dying at sea. My friend called it "moving
in for the killed." She was probably talking
about men.

The best staircases are spiral. For to venture
Upward or downward is to venture in many directions.
But if the nothing-ventured is an outcast, so also
is the adventurer beyond roots. But for sure
the facts the numbers and the sweat bring us
not much nearer to the almighty intuition,
let alone make us pious. They are also merely
true.
Last night all that seemed as clear as a glass.

And I think I ordered her to understand it.
And I think the sea she was as yellow as glass
as I died and roared
              and rose like a mountain within her

Yet now in this hovel --
One woman's act of home,
Upon this far from level bed,
I need how to pray; for one moment --
                for one fact of my own --
For one head to live it with.

I get down on my knees
                Like an insect in the dark. O Sareth,

(O heaven-given harpooner from Nazareth)
How soon can I know? O say
                With what hunger can I be fed

THE smell of mango season
Little Violet fruit-bound mud-green
Her grin grown to a near-toothless portal
Wattled-in

The drizzle and the bus blowin
Stream stroking the trash-roofs . . .

STRETCHING her face
my friend makes an industry of her mouth
and of her eyes
Stumbles out
soaking among the files

stretches her hips:

                                              (St. Vincent, 6 June 1947)

## ADEYEMI

*(a legend of kinship)*

A Man set out to Ibadan
and arrive at Cologne

One day he met his brother's mother
Singing OMOYA for his mother's son

Another day he look for blood
The same day she look for everything

The next he look for proper green pepper
The same day she look for a name
for everything he looking for
from thorn-crowns to gold-holes
and palm-bone and red-beans
and double-barrel madness in old
Sierra Leone

The very next day she give him hand-woven
soup and love-cloth from Mende
and a sap-proud song that every Sunday
she addressed
to her land-rover son Gaston-Bart-Williams
her very own
raised in Sierra Leone
Just like Johann-Sebastien-Beethoven-
(to-name-three-of-the-best)

At midnight he cursed her son
Put westindian sugar-blood in her soup

And she heeded him and fed him

Because she could not bear it

Early next morning
Sing OMOYA
Inside that charm of bones and everything
lying down among her very own things
from palm-history to mother-bones
from mother-woven days
double-barrel mende clothes
from love and Afrika and everything
Bearing his blood and proper proper crown
she named him

### ADEYEMI

So now dear mother
and all dear mother sons
OMOYA and good morning

Your crown fit me so I wear it

(London, 14 April 1973)

## LOVE STORY (13)

TAKE me to arms
       And I will have to hold you
Trouble me and teach me

      Take me into your sleep

Starve me
And I will feast upon you

      Church me
           To worship you

Hold me    Hold me
      And I will have to take you

      Take me to house
      And I will feast sleep and dwell
            starve nibble and worship with you

      Take me to battle
      And I will have to kill you

(St. Vincent, 17 December 1976)

## PEANUTS -- 1946

*(for Kathie and Cecil Cyrus, and for Carmelle)*

Shelling out our hearts like peanuts
blowing away together the red chaff

                            you can't eat

we would walk all the way
from huts of Sion Hill
to the palace of Fort Charlotte -- and back again --
about ten miles -- or nine steps
if it was Friday and moonlight.

Once she asked me
if I thought the moon was a harlot
just because she gave herself to everybody
I choked   and felled her hastily
with a kiss
just to see if she tasted the same.
Some Friday nights it was like this
though we were inclined
not to remember.

In old Cary Wilson's cinema -- (theatre)
She held me very close by the little finger
while Humphrey Bogart smelled something or other
or Buck Jones or Tom Keen
wasted their time with horses and guns.
And one night in the Park
when she turned to me in the dark
and asked me to feel for maybe a hairpin

                            she had lost

I choked and thanked God.
(Earlier she had wished me luck
for the Cambridge Higher School Certificate
coming up in December).

These things somehow remind me
that bananas can be eaten
without thinking about the world market
and lovers' mothers can be helped
                            to decorate a church
at harvest
and politics may be more or less
what you hear on the B.B.C. Overseas Service.

One Friday night when it was like that
we heard that huts and palaces never meet
for long . . .

SHELLING peanuts today
with hardly anyone to help blow away
the dead stuff you can't eat
I am inclined
to doubt certain things
about bananas and the B.B.C.
and Fort Charlotte and things . . .

And I am sure
it being such a long time since I realized
that all my loose talk
about wanting more
than little-finger walks and peanut skies
did not in the least deceive her,
that my sailing far away

on that empty Sunday morning
never did quite display
    how bravely I could leave her.

(Bequia, 29 December 1976)

## LOVE STORY (1)

        You're
          a
        poet

    I know it

                                          run

   I'm

a

    poet

                                              it's fun

come

                        now we're a poet

            do we know it

                                      (St. Vincent, 30 June 1977)

## ONE WOMAN

" . . . for me
it only have **one** Woman
in this world
>you hear

It must be have
donkey thousand kind o' man
but only **one woman** for me

It have        -- yo know me father a'ready --
>lemme see

boat-man    goat-man    flirty-man    dutty-man
   seine-man    caneman    brainman    politician

MAN

>all kind o' man
>
>>you hear
>
>hen-man      fren-man      pan-man
>gun-man
>>dons-an'-run-man
>>>woman
>
>All kind
>
>But only but ONE    ONE    **WOMAN**

And da's M Y M O T H E R
A true yellow woman-carib

And only death -- could kill she
>>SO
>>you best had
>>DON'T EVEN CALL SHE NAME . . .

(St. Vincent, 1976)

## LOVE STORY (3)

    . . . Because
    my mistress did not hesitate
I told her to feel free
to love me as she wished

She replied
    If you should wish to love me
as freely as I am loving you
you have only to let our love
enslave you

It was thus
    that I despoiled her
and became her mistress for many years

(St. Vincent, 1976)

## NOTHING VENTURED

Daily sort of day

not much used

dusty

clouds crisp
now rust-brown
no work of art

door open
closed it

young people eating
smelling of fat she said

we ordered
or rather
she ordered

the waitress dipped
just like that

moved away

my 14$^{th}$ wife had accused me

no proof

three slice of bread-pudding
were laid
before the woman before me

Clouds were crisp
now soft

rained only on this roof
door closed

I too
soft
light-strained
soundless
under crust

From her first bite
I know
something important
would be denied me

no proof

my 14th had asked
for 15 days to reconsider

the waitress dipped
towards our table
crisp and claw-fingered
tart

At that moment
it was possible to estimate
that the one before me
the woman
my 14th
would dispose of the pudding
in about fifteen bites

(St. Vincent, 25 July 1979)

## LOVE STORY (21)

No one
ever looks at
the face
of a nun

                      or the face of a whore
Do crabs in motion masturbate

           Wherever there's a high place
install a gun

    I could die
loving you

Darkness and thistles surround my face like the sun

There are very few nuns in China

         When thorns are set to mate
         the roses run
               More and more
    virgin islands will be born as oceans defecate

   Jack loves Joan who loves John
Shake loves Shama who loves the son of man

        Guns move backwards
        when they speak

In June the days dilate
        and you are here in my arms in a high place
            crabs mimic thorns
        muddle and run
        celebrate among the roses

>   love leaks from the island of the sun
>   the whole down-thrust evening hesitates

Soon you will lie backwards
>   and say
>   it's too dark
>   and in any case too late to notice my face

I love you

(St. Vincent, 13 September 1977)

## LOST AND FOUND LOST

AFTER love
is lost
      he-Man
will butcher
the rest
of the world
to recover
the image
of his
lover

he will remove
an arm
from one woman
breasts
from another
a style
of laughter
from another
even plunder
a syllable
or a habit of thought
in the
effort
to reconstruct
the myth
and the beauty
of his
lost love

every woman he meets and knows
will contribute that part
of herself
which contributes towards
the architecture of HER memory

and after
he has dismembered
many
he will
perhaps
be exhausted
sundered
by search
or
he will be discovered by
or discover
  she-Woman
who
is
a
new
and wholly sweet construction

who is enough
who is enough

whose parts
he cannot
persuade
or phase
singly

into the image
of another

whom his memory cannot dissect
whom he fears
into whom he grows
who is his myth
whom he will challenge
curious to hate
desperate to renounce
whom he loves

AFTER love
       is lost
              she-Woman
     will butcher
the rest of the world . . .

                                                     (St. Vincent, 1952-1977)

BOOK THREE

# THIRTEEN STUDIES IN HOME ECONOMICS

St. Vincent, 1972 - 1977

*All the world's a casino.*
*The particular world into which I was born --*
*Or deliver, if you prefer -- is over sixty miles long, and*
*some eleven miles wide. North to south*
*You can play any number of games from Fancy to Union.*
*The west and east walls are know as Barrouallie and Stubbs Point respectively . . .*

*For decoration we have a volcano smoking away peacefully at four thousand feet.*
*But the rest of the place is almost always real high . . .*

*Wall to wall refreshment area is about*
*one hundred and fifty square miles, providing us with*
*thousands and thousands of digging space acreage --*
*fertile and well soaked -- capable of producing anything*
*except principles.*

## (Lesson One:     FAMILY FIGGERS)

        2 into 1
        yo can't
        **borry** 0
        2 into 10 equals 5

        5 into 1 yo can't
        **beg** for 0
        yo can't but
        5 into 10 equals 2

and 2 into 2 yo can
    So **steal** 1

        yo can't

(Cologne, February 1972)

**(Lesson Two:     OPTIONS)**

A MANICOU woke up one morning
Look at his shadow
And thought
I am going to have a breadfruit for lunch today.

At midday
He looked again at his shadow
And thought
A guava will do.

Next morning
He woke up and thought
Today I must have two breadfruit for lunch
And he looked at his shadow.

At midday he looked again at his shadow

(St. Vincent, 16 August 1973. Adapted from Kahlil Gibran)

**(Lesson Three: PAPA AMOEBA)**

**BUT listen Mum**
**Who made Caricom**

Island commodities child
(I mean communities)
You and me and the future
Is Um

**B -b -b - but Mum**
**Who made the past then**

**Mum**
**Where it come from**

Child
Listen chile
The amoeba is de past
Just like yo father
De father of Evolution
Amoeba is Um
It have a private nucleus
And a public protoplasm
(But Mum, Mum, Mum . . . ) . . .
      And when it have a urge
To multiply

It does divide

**Part II. (optional)**

      Just like yo father
      Just like Carry Come

**But Mum**
**When de future going to come.**
**I mean like you and me**
**Sugar flour all and some**
**Happy things**
**Agro-culture goodhardwork and rum**
**Mum**

Child
Trust yo mother love yo father
But

Every hour
Dividing every hour
I wonders
Just like you
Where Papa Amoeba come from.

(St. Vincent, 10 May 1974)

**(Lesson Four: MATURITY)**

NOBODY DOESN'T SUPPOSE

TO STAN-UP PON NO STREET CORNER

    LOOKIN LEF AN RIGHT

                 18 CENTS A NIGHT

    LEF AND RIGHT

        DON'T KNOW      DON'T KNOW

    **WHAT THE SHITE**

SPECIALLY WHEN THAT BODY

    IS 18 YEARS

THE AGE OF MATURITY

           **Sign by hand**
           **This 24 night of march 1975**

                  **N O B O D Y.**

(St. Vincent, 27 March 1975)

(Lesson Five:        PER CAPITA PER ANNUM)

Number of people under review --
 91000. Percentage of invisible fathers
  or mothers of haphazard status --
   79. (or more). Number of people
    who pay taxes -- too many
     or too few. Number of people
      who starve; number of people who
      eat; number of people
       who eat people who starve . . .
         Number of humans, hybrids,
           hermaphrodites,
            hominids . . .

**hogsheads of hate**
**still wait to be opened**
**in the headquarters of the hungry**

Number of large heads, spring beds
 large bellies, distended guts, percentage
 of placentas per square-inch of a
  school-yard; estimate of prostitutes
   per public-centimeter of a cradle.
     Number of beggars, wooden legs,
       scrunters, hunters, highest-
         common-factor of broken skulls
          per milli-litre of strong rum;
           of broken hearts per man-hour
            of gossip, percentage of
              sheep per driver . . .

**in heaven in 1976
there were thousands of suicides
who giggled**

Estimates of imports in proportion to bans
 on imports; gross shipping in proportion
  to fishing boats per hundred; cares
   in proportion to arise-holes of population;
    makes of cars, number of types
     of number-plates of cars.
      Visitors who cannot relate to home,
       divided by tourist who cannot
        pay
         to leave home.
          Vice against vaccinations,
           lawyers against builders,
          dreams
            against people
             who cannot sleep . . .

**then there was feasting
in the streets of Kush
when the last slave
returned healthy with treasure
from Taiwan**

Percentage of decibels to blossoms;
 number of quiet people, fearless people;
  number of people decently assaulted
   by other people; square-roots of gardens
    inhabited by paranoid mongrels,
     percentage of poems

>> damaged in transport,
>> act of love and labour
>> accurately recognizable
>> as pleasure . . .

**everyone remembers
not a single song
of the Callinagos**

Graphs to indicate the upward and downward
   curve of arrowroot; segments
   of social circles removed by surgery.
      Emergency graves for the heads
         of stolen cattle.
            Straw hats and straw mats;
               hundreds of people
                  with rock-faces fishing for status;
                  nine people fishing
                     with rods on rocks
                        with lanterns
                           ole mas' faces
                              lights without luster
                                 crabs . . .

**but I could name you
by name
the first Spaniard
who vomited into his guitar**

182000 noseholes under review.
   Hunters and scrunters too many or
      too few. Petites of baby-killing semen;
         popcorn; popsicles

> with number-plates;
> the downward curve of pigeon-peas,
> poems, cognition and recognition
> that died thrashing
> in an abandoned
> ambulance . . .

**when I was a child
you could buy Aztec soulfood
outside the temple of Nineveh**

Numbers of numbers --
   bers, bers, blurs, -- NUMB, -- oh so numb . . .
    Exodus, Leviticus, numbers,
     levies, lies, lassitudes . . .

Numberless people under review.
   Number of THEM -- 91000.
    Number of US -- 91000.
      Till death
        give us a head-start --
        per capita
        per annum
        every year
        HERE . . .

**during
next lesson
Lesson Six
those who so wish
will be taught how to count**

(St. Vincent, 21 June 1975)

**(Lesson Six: HOW TO COUNT)**

One

two

three

four

      five

and

so

on

      up

      to

      nought

Repeat **r e s o l u t e l y**

until

you're

caught

**(Lesson Seven: CREDENTIAL)**
*(for **Shadow**, a modern kaisonian)*

SIX year ole

an' me farder gimme a trumpit

an' 'e show me

how to blow it

how to polish it

how to respec' it

An' 'e say

                    exercise yo potential

Hold on to dis

But de neighbour-dem say
Bwoy wheh yo manners
Wheh yo wool-tie
Wheh yo hymnbook an' yo cork-hat
Yo mean yo farder didn't gie yo dat? . . .

                    **So Ah try out me credential**
                    **Ah tek it out**
                    **an' Ah polish it**
                    **an' dey like it**
                    **an' Ah say**
                    **Me farder didn' gie me dat**
                    **But 'e gimme dis**

Eighteen year ole
An' me girlfrien' vex wid me trumpit

She say

     bwoy wheh you money
wheh yo hard-pants
wheh yo whisky an yo shut-jack an yo Fiat
dat is essential
udderwise you gwine miss

                        tit fe tat

                So Ah roll-up me credential
                We repolish it
                then Ah   **blow-it**
                an' she like it
                an' Ah say
                Me farder didn' gimme dat
                But  'e gie we
                Dis

Twenty-five year ole
An' Ah hit de mudder-country
An' Ah show dem all me manners and me certifikiss

But de trouble me
She

                bwoy wheh yo histry
                where your culture
                wheh yo farder
                where your money and your hot-shirt
                where your felt-hat . . .

**Ah say no profit no potential in dis**

**So   Ah tek out me essential**

**an'  Ah polish it**

> **an' dey respec' it**
> **an' So dey respec' it So Ah blow it**
> **An' Ah say**
> **Is me farder wha' gimme dat**
> **An' wha' gimme**
> **Dis**

Forty year ole
an' Ah touch back down 'pon me country
an' Ah like it
an' Ah cool it
an' Ah bring back all me farder trumpit
gie dem

But de sweet fool-dem say
    bwoy **What** yo come for
wheh yo big car
wheh yo wool-hat
wheh yo snap-soul an' yo whiskey an' yo 'tankerousniss
All-we culture all-we potential
is definightly non-residential
all dis trumpit is a famous load o' piss

                      hold on to dis

> So Ah hice up me credential
> same one wha' me farder show
> how fe polish
> how fe respec'
> how fe blow
> an' Ah say..// ¾! Sxhf=+f@@@...

(St. Vincent, 25 June 1976)

**(Lesson Eight:     HERE AM I SEND ME)**

bottles
nipples

topless
playthings
in
the
ice-box
        in
        the
        cive-patch

a bird
spins around
brought
down
by
a
foul
wind

lice
in the carrot patch
tongues
crooked and brown
like a doormat

no
juice
brings up
the young ox

a bell
bang

glad to be of use
when
they
die
or reproduce . . .

                How many here can eat my rice

a bat
hangs
between
the nipple
   and
      the left ventricle

lice
all over the bird in the ice -- box
white

like

jesuschrist
 ice

on

my

wing

                                (St. Vincent, 18 June 1976)

**(Lesson Nine:     UNDERWATER GAMES)**

They came up at last
for a holiday
he and his country both
or for breath as you might say
      they were drowning

The second time
they tried to tackle the work
even make a sort of love
renaming the game
      it was late

Even if the tide turned
it would leave them gazing
only at what they might have made

a little saving of water
in a hollow of mud
a little blood

The third time
they were too busy breathing

Yet if at last the common air
seemed not much to speak of
perhaps one of them
could lift a bloody hand
to hack and heckle and make history
as it were
      games often end
      like this
Since water

is not industrial
he could not understand
where the knives came from
or why they came
at his neck and side

he simply died
       it was amazing

(St. Vincent, 23 June 1975)

(Lesson Ten:    MAN ABOUT THE HOUSE)

### (a) Bringing up a dog (a statement of my 50th birthday)

FIRST you must name it well --
for example, "Nutmeg" --
> (blackest-born of "Peanut" -- how did you guess? --
> father uncertain -- a distant compelling fiction) . . .

Try to signify
something possible to process,
the sort of personality you could sell easily
                            in a bag.

Then you must feed it well --
condition powder, dumplings, coconut shell;
a little water -- preferably stale --
will make it need you.
If you're going to clip its tail
do it early
       otherwise it will wag.

**All these things must be tastefully done
with the help of friends . . .
And you must be firm.**

Be most careful how you choose its friends.
To do this well
you must reject as dangerous and confusing
anything that laughs, is too quiet,
or likes choosing,
or christables;   or seems

attracted to you, your house, your garden,

your private dreams . . .

**All this must be done by conviction.**

(Dogs
do it mostly by smells)

Its formal education will depend on how well
you can manipulate
the virtue of going mad --
the chain, the scratch on the head,
the even-handed torture
                with a piece of old rag . . .

Useful also to tell yourself daily
that  gratitude is a virtue
of which soul-hunger is the main pre-condition;
eager to learn
       that all good children
       are good,
       do not bit unless they are bitten to,
       and do not go to hell.

All good dogs are bad . . .

**These things have all been done**
                **without indecent waste, and well,**
**almost to the point of addiction, --**

And my masters tell me
                I am in excellent condition,

     though from time to time I smell

            out of turn . . .
                             like hell

## (b) Next to godliness

ONE morning
while
digging out
weeds
from a drain
I
   pick myself
     up
       by the tail
   and thought
    Goodheavens
it's
alive

     Several days later
cleaning a window against the light
an early moth picked me up
by the tips of its wings

     I'm alive

         Good Heavens

(St. Vincent, 30 May 1977)

**(Lesson Eleven: WHO'S YO FATHER)**

       MULE
              is we people
     e aint fish e aint fowl
e wukkin e wukkin e wukkin
  e kickin up e kickin up

              e ears l o n g

but e cant hear e own story

furthermore

             e cant     propagate

e knoweth nothing name future

EVERY new generation
is some body haffo find horse and donkey
      fo start off MULE all over again    /MULE

                        (St. Vincent, 5 November 1977)

## (Lesson Twelve:   MY NEIGHBOUR PLUM TREE)

I WATCHIN it
    every day I watchin it
it growin nice yes all right it growin nice

    BUT
        my nerves
cant stan the way he and he wife
        spennin so much time
pon a simple ting like a plum tree

I mean
    sometime of a SUNDAY mornin
she does come out the house early early
    befo cock even start bury fowl
steps out of the house
        in she short short nightie
stoops down by da plum tree
        meddlin-up the dirt round it
say she **manurin** it

        only showin off she ting
        like-a ripe plum

**Hmmm**

I remember
    the Satday mornin
        she mudder bring the plum tree
    just a teeny-weeny cuttin with no leaf
        without nothin mark plum pon it

I remember how they laughin

        and skinnin up they teet
    while **all-o-dem** plantin it

but **he**
    is the one meks the most style
                with da plum tree

like I mean
    when a man come home from wuk
do he have any callin to leap out he car
    even befo the moto stop run
        an is so he feelin up the tree
    fingerin up all the bottom leaf
    and the top leaf
        lovin dem up
            touchin dem up
                muchin dem up

**plum tree leaf**    I tell you

I does have to say like **dis** plum tree ha bubby and backside

**Hmmm**

and the little darn boney-neck chile they have
    does even tell the tree goodmornin
like if she want tun it stupid

    yo wouldn believe me but
even the dorg        does manure dat tree

**Hmmm**

y e s

    it growin nice

I don't say nothin wrong wid that
>anything name tree
>>suppose to grow

but dem          and they car          and they boney-neck . . .

**Hmm**

>I wonder
>>how **she** mudder
>>come by a piece of plum tree cuttin

everybody know she live in the middle of bottom town
>where it don't evenself ha grass
>>much less plum tree
>>>she must be tief it . . .

>>>>**Hmmm**

. . . and it aint he one have car
>I ha car too

I get it same week he get his own

I don't look for the wuk yet
to put in a steering wheel into it but don't you mind

I have my two eyes in me head
>and my sense
>>so nobody cant stop me from siddown
>>>by my darn own window
>>and watch any ting I want to watch...

(Sh . . . Sh . . . She and she blasted plum Hmmmmmm)
I bet you
>they must be does dream bout when the plum tree bear
>how all the likkle children round here

gwine flock by **fodem** house
>    and call dem mister and mistress
>    and beg them please to have couple grain of plum

Sir

    y e s

I watchin it it growin nice

But le me tell you something

Jus   leh  da  plum  tree

Only grow ONE INCH

>    faster than mines

**Hmmm**

(St. Vincent, 4 November 1977)

**(Lesson Thirteen: SONG OF THE UNDERDEVELOPED CASINO)**

TEN GREEN BOTTLES
STANDING ON A WALL
*(Repeat)*

**If by Chance**
One of them should fall, . . .
"And if by **Chance**
we should find each other, -- it's beautiful"[1] . . .
**What a horrible way to start a relationship,
Especially with another person!**

Anyway, baby, let's just you and me
and the six other mystery-chance-takers
just bingo on down
to the St. Ives Turf Club
where the action only costs a dollar . . .
      **Only a dollar it corss?!**
Well, if so, there will be

TEN GREEN BOTTLES
STANDING ON A WALL
*(Repeat)*

And if perchance any of them should fall,
Well, I mean to say,
If a woman or her man should gain
the whole world and lose their true over-proof spirits,
Where is the profit therein?
              For we have written

      **From the poor**

> **shall be taken away**
> **even that which**
> **they doth not have**

So
sweet citizens of St Ives
there may always be

TEN GREEN BOTTLES
STANDING ON A WALL
*(Repeat)*

Well, it befell one day,
at the end of the family-planning seminar,
"each delegate was presented with a plague
in the shape of St Vincent" . . .
(Cited out of context from the *Vincentian* newspaper) --

> **One shelf-load of self-employed contraceptive**
> **tablets to the first 1000 young people who**
> **spot the misprint.**

The winners
are asked to keep their eyes on the

TEN GREEN BOTTLES
STANDING ON A WALL.
*(Repeat)*

> And I do suppose
> Humpty-Dumpty would fall out with me
> if I told him
> that I have many sisters
> who regularly lose forty skins a week
> playing dominoes with Teacher . . .

I am their keeper . . .
They have to call my mother   Mother . . .

And another thing
baby girl, baby boy,
All this world is a casino.

Bahamo
        Acapulco
                Monaco
                        Pennistino

You just name it, and AWAY WE GO.
After all
The man Shakespeare said so . . .

And I remember the time
when my mother
who was the 1927 "Teen-age Mother of the year"
presented her 23 children
to the parent-teachers' association.
        On that occasion
all of us children
were signed up in advance
as senior black-jack dealers
in the Langley park Sugar-Dream Casino . . .

The Principal commended her
on the excellent way
she had brought up her offspring.
For it was then revealed
that my mother had always insisted
that all her children
have to call each others' fathers

Uncle . . .
just to make sure that there are

TEN GREEN BOTTLES
STANDING ON A WALL.
*(Repeat)*

Ten     very     green mothers
taking chances on a wall

And if by CHANCE
the whole bloody lot of us should fall
you can bet your ole soul
your ole bingo-blasted soul
your ole chance-worshipping, father-masquerading,
come-and-get-it-because-you-didn't-work-for-it,
freeness-enterprised
underdeveloped ole soul,
      There will always be

TEN GREEN BOTTLES
Repeat    Green
    GR    EEE    NNNNN
              G    R    E    E    N

GR e e   n

        grrrrr . . . . . .

(St. Vincent, 26 June 1977)<br>Disco-poet, Copyright 1973, Velvet Screen Enterprises.

BOOK FOUR

# **PALM AND OCTOPUS**
Twelve Love Poems

September 1994
Brooklyn, New York

*To Chris, long promised.*

## BANANAS

Whole bananas
load me to where
you are not
when I sprout with growing
towards you

Tomorrow you will be Gone old
with chemicals
and other hands
towards
another place
another Race
another race
another signal of unknown
distress

Yesterday
I hoped I would grow
towards you
you and me towards

I strive now
to hold on to the wind
to the tree of your green
green late and gone

Every day
you come back to me
like early sunshine
too late unknown
too late in time

For you
have exported me
washed and green
 chemical
clean and frozen
to another clime.

## DANCE FOR ME

Dance for me
as you spread your hips
around my life

and my lips
answer to a life
I need to know

And why am I so cautious
of the indications
of your present
and my eyes
and my past growing

to a place
where you
and the dance
and the music
strike me down
as a nomination for love

And nowhere else is there
such a dance
is there such love

## RISE UP WITHIN ME

and lie down
like a torch at rainbow time
full of oil
full of fuel
full of my rightful destination

You can drain out
the whole of my history
through the scorn
of your eyes
and the fingertips of temptation
when our thighs are old
and crusted
like palm trees
on dead December mornings

But oil flows slowly
yearly and yellow
as a rainbow glows yellow
after rain

As dawn arches downward to dusk
is encrusted with darkness
and is gone

## TWO YEARS AGO

Two years ago
finally talked to you

baffled me
with the speed of your sunlight

Last year
lay beside you
as the moon of your mouth
made me hear yes and no
in a light of careful dreams
long ago

Tonight something
croon I something
about yes and no
wondering if you know
I have learned to talk you out of sight

(One day I will write something about this)

## THERE WAS NOT

There was not
a lot
of space
in the grass between
the road and the turn of the river

Why did we go walking
on such a night
a night pursued by rain

There was not a lot of space
where damp old worms burrowed and behaved
and quiet and cramped it was
between our thighs and the thunder

It rained why & why & why
and why
did you flow
quietly away with the river

Why do I pretend
that the grass
like a memory thundering under me
is still green

## IN THIS ANCIENT BAY

In this ancient bay
vessels move as one
mounting the swell
haunches taut
hair undone

In this ancient bay
clouds haunt mountains
mountains
seem to grope upwards among clouds
in small rhythms
gross-green like the vessels

In some ancient bay
I am still hoping
to find you

## SINGING THIS MORNING

Singing this morning
rose in my rags
like a sacrament

knowing you have promised
to meet me
at the appointed time
of our crucifixion

knowing we shall die together
at our appointed time
near the noise of rivers
near flourishing flowers

holding   hissing   hoping
moaning   confessing
our new time

Who cares
about the happiness of others

How can we not rage in our rags
reckless and right
and sacred for all time

## AND WILL YOU
*(With some help from Gerard Manley Hopkins)*

Touch me again afresh
as words touch the tongue
and many times over again
as hair touches the air
art touches the eyes
as nothing touches nothing
as houses touch
as darlings touch
as the womb touches the child

As words toughen the page
as music touches a drum
as age may touch the young

As everything touches nothing
as sometimes all things touch
as tears touch laughter
baldness the bare head
ashes the dead
boldness and fear those in love

I swear I have dreamed how
to touch you with my love

Over again I feel thy finger and find thee

## YOU WILL REMEMBER

You will remember
how I asked you to fall from a high place
in Chateaubelair
to prove you loved me
      And you said your daughter would suffer
alone    and your grandmother would starve
and if you died you could not possibly know
if I had been joking    or if
I would fall after you
and love you in death on the rocks below
and leave our child to starve
without us

      That night there was a lonely fisherman
on the rocks below
with a lantern and a bamboo rod
fishing  (wife and children no doubt)

    He heard us talking
His rod was bent with a new fish

He had a light

                      He heard us talking

## PALM AND OCTOPUS

Hardly a day passes
that I do not regret
having told you
how much I love you

Because you are a palm tree
beautiful
and rigid rooted

And I an octopus
flailing at food
eight arms
nomadic in water

Each today after eleven years
I remember our death before it happens
and who knows what other green things will reach me
with watery tendrils of love

Yet I think of you
as we might have been
grey scales green hair
and water far far from our liquid thoughts

**FROGS**

Male frogs
live upon the backs of female frogs
waiting for her eggs to appear
and his sperm to touch them   make them whole

Ants in season mate on the wings

Some woman spiders kill the man
eat him  right after mating

Nourishment is always for the young

People have no wings

Girl blackbirds demand food
from boy blackbirds in the season

Put your clothes on and have another drink . . .
What's that you said
       I said
              Do we always have to talk about such things?

## I NEED TO APOLOGIZE

for having lived

                so long

      Did not mean to trouble you
           with this part of my life

You too

Your laughter reaches me
        uncertainly
               like the tentacles of a palm tree
                  like our silhouettes
                      in the river
                                water pursuing water

Later today my love it will rain

BOOK FIVE

# THE WISDOM-KEEPERS

THREE POEMS LOCATED IN THE VOICE OF THE TEA-MEETIN,
THE KAISO, THE FOLK (JUMBIE) METAPHYSIC, AND
OTHER TRADITIONAL LANGUAGE FORMS

St. Vincent, 1972-1974

## NANCITORI
*(for Daniel Williams)*

I THINK I SHALL SURELY DIE
OF STARVATION said Poopa Nanci
one day to him wife; for the
POLITICAL SITUATION IS WEARY
FENCED IN WITHOUT AND WITHIN
the banana dem down with blight
and the flies are thin I AM TALKIN
TO YOU MISTRESS NANCI

Mistress Mother Nanci was also
ripe with starvation, so too
the three children, February and March
Nanci, not forgetting April Nanci
who was the youngest and a girl.
      Mooma Nanci, ripe and thoughtful
with hungry said, "Husband mine,
I am starvin thinkin of the children
I had a dream of Asante last night
and in my dream
Rope say is better hang than starve."

                              (HERE NARRATOR SINGS)

     NANCI, who smells of palmolive oil
And absinthe, who beat a lion in a race
from Togo to Guanahani, Nanci
who knows everything from Troy to
Tensing, and who has once been
carved in ivory by Jamaican Namba Roy

as a gift for the princess lady, Margrit English,
who not withstanding that he knows well
how to stand starved upon a plinth
was dying for hungry, said:

(SONG FROM CHORUS)

"Wife? Mooma Mistress, not forgetting
the children, lookit here,
that which you say concerning hope
I mean rope
Do you remember friend brother
Toucouma? Whose tail is long like rope
but differently succulent?   Tasteful, bwoy,
and against starvation. I think
we shall eat it
February March or April. We are hungry
from Chile to Swahili. My Namba
I will took it"

(HERE APRIL BRIEFLY SINGS)

"YOU and the children will cook it."

"GOOD morning Brother Toucouma
how are you abiding I trust you are aware
of pollution over Canaan and Missolonghi
and Florida continues to piss cultural waste
upon the Caribbean where I and you is now
residing
You have a fine tail there."

    "Good morning Poopa Nanci
February March and April the young girl
Not forgetting. What is your solution."

"Good morning friend Toucouma, the execution
of my journey twixt Togo and here, Doku and Namba
starvation and story is nigh I mean near.
You are my solution."

(HERE NARRATOR SINGS)

**Nanci now negotiating Toucouma tc a swimmin race**
**For soothing him nerves and exposing disgrace**
**Form the world situation.**
**Toucouma tempted by pride and haste and fancy**
**For appropriating history and world concept**
**To dispose Nanci and all his face**
**To impose humiliation**
**And bury his mace**
**In April's taste**
**Accept the race.**

Hear nanci now, nuh:
"Brother friend Tookooks I know you are the best
Swimmer in the Atlantic and I am only
Spider Ananse web-plasterer from Kumasi
(But the best). Who can surpass me
Providing you are fair and not unfair?
I have only legs but you have four legs
And a tail so I beseech you
Right here on Hairoun beach to take off
Your tail and leave it here in hiding
In sight of all and in the name of fairity
Then we can begin our famous race."

"Poopa friend Nancilings begorra and His Blood
We will swim this contest from here to Hewanorra

I tookooks Toucouma am leastways the best
Swimmer in the west.  And the fairest on four legs.
And the hexecution of my fairity is here and there
For all to see.  If I set my face to France
Is April will be my destination.  And the starvation
of the fierceliness and pride of such fancilings
As you is always my concern without fail
Let the race begin.  Let us swim . . .
Here is my tail."

    WELL SIR
Toucouma leave him tail on the beach
And six legs plus four legs clever as ever
The race begin.

                           (HERE SINGS APRIL A SONG)

Tookooks send himself
Like a streak of wire
In the water and begorra
Just as you say pharaoh's daughter he done leave
All politics behind him
Breasting and besting all the way
From Hairoun to Hewanorra
And he swim
Like a arrow don't tricks don't tire don't bend.

And Nanci?

Well before yo belly go buss wid laugh
He naturally only dip down him nose
in the water
Come back bubblin
To the beach

Clip up Toucouma tail
Decompose
The whole situation
From dublin to pithecanthropus
And before
You can holler SHAME
CULTURATION
They done cookup nyamup the man tail
    And is so they heng up and curl up
Five furl up full-belly spider
Up in the roof of the polluted world
Jam up like island
Waitin for Toucouma to come back and CLAIM.

                          (HERE SOME CHILDREN SING)

**POOPA LOOK**
**Toucouma come back for him tail.**

                                 (APRIL SINGS)

**Nancitori family**
**Creole shanty show**
**Heng up in the roof of the world**
**Toucouma down below**
**Absent palm oil know**
**Where Juba and Joliba flow**
**Mouth open big**
**And slow**
**Like the family history of the world**
**Ashanti 'Nanse Spider**
**Family swingin to and fro**
**In the everlooted Congo**

**Of the world**

FEBRUARY START TO SAY
    Mooma I weary I want to drop
Mooma Mistress Nanci say
    Look 'im day
    February, Look Toucouma down below;
    The man wid no tail will eat you so.
February groan
    Mooma I weary what you have to say

MOOMA SAY:

    **Bwoy, I love the man from Accompong**
    **But I pity the man who always find a way**

    **So tell yo Poopa**

Hear February again, nuh:
    Poopa I weary
Nanci sing:
    **Well drop then.**

Toucouma below appropriates history in his maw.
Canaan and Guyana negotiate the law
Of the polluted world.

                (ALL HERE COME NEAR TO A SONG)

March sings
    Mooma I weary
    **Tell yo Poopa**
    Poopa I weary

    **Well drop then, Tookooks down below.**

ALL OF A SUDDEN SO

MOOMA NANCI SELF SING OUT

### Darlin Tookooks I weary

Tell yo husban

**APRIL the oldest face in the world**
**Dimple gape and suckle of many worlds**
**Looked at the raping and the waiting down below**
**In the end grew weary told her father so**

Poopa Nanci say:
    "To rawtid to fuckle and to rarse
I am a weary father        a weary father
And may soon be diving
To Toucouma soon soon   TOUCOUMA   you are excellent
And a friend
And you know

      The law of swimming and surviving --
The different succulences of all who pray
For mercy in your maw and for reviving . . .
BUT the fancy of your fairity is without surpass
Notwithstanding that you did not win the Spider
In that famous race from San Christobal
To Mango     I mean Rangoon

Here is my solution:

      "You know how my daughter discretely furnish
(And the banana root dem blighted like matches
will soon meet their hour)
      Do not de-loot history of her nourishment
If you don't wish her sweetness to splatter away
And go undeavour

Spread nine bags of ashes on the floor
Whereon she will drop
So she will fall secretly and soft and more
Compose for your accomplishment."

**GRANNY DEAR**
**Toucouma find himself**
**Tempted another time by pride**
**And haste to be appropriating**
**To bind his face in April's ligament**
**Speard more**
**Than nine bags of ashes on the floor**

(HERE ALL SING)

And
The last I heard of this ditty of mine was that
April drop in the ashes
And swinghin Bredda Toucouma done roar away
Hoppin creazy firin like mathces
And pretty sure blind with the ashes stinghin up
His eye like jack spaniar poultice or nettie pie
Down to the grinnin grey horizontal sea
And April Nanci
     Are alive and well
If you don't like my story you can go to hell
Neither if you don't like my tale you can go
To jail this is my romance
And if it don't sweet you you can go to france

For the wire done bend
And the story end

(Cologne, 11 August 1972)

## KAISO KAISO

It have
so much reason why
woman santapee
must more than bad
So man santapee
learn to do sand-dance
and fireman and so
Without no sensation
they cause a consternation
forty days and forty nights
all down Wrightson road
And all Tunapuna
turn inside out
**in the lenten season!**

Woman santapee
supposes
to more worserer than bad
so nobody frighten
nobody sad
when she swip sheself
inside me tent
**in the lenten season!**
excite me whole temptation
inside out
Me and me fireman rhythm
strengthening for the season

posing all down Dry River
passing the bamboo

and the tambu
Aaks we we intention
and the whole population
sing
because
some-o'-dem someting
is sweeter than someting

It don't have so much
reason why
when the boys come out to play
mother telling daughter
daughter telling friend
watch you tray-lay-lay
run a mile and a half
**and aaks when what is their intention**
They will dazzle reason in you eye
and sting yo like a sting-a-ray

**Sandimanite**

Child
is why you winding up so
The teacher say
yo singing

forty night
and forty day
bout the creature
from the black lagoon
Don't you care bout yo lessons
don't you care
Don't you learn yet

how to rhyme
Don't your future waiting
in the kaskadura
Don't you care
what the creature do you
down by the river
inside the black lagoon
You think is three four time
Kitchener have to rhyme

Child don't you care to learn
how santapee can tell the time
and the whole population turn
tremendous incarnation
while you sit down dey
only playing with yo tray-lay-lay
papa pays as he earn
Cousin gone fishening
for fish in the lenten season
Pussy has finish
his work for the day
and the little mice beating
a tremendous palpitation
up and down the sweeping broom
Fowl and santapee sleeping
upsided down
while future boys come out to play
beside our black lagoon

**Aaks them what is their intention**

Jackfish frying
but the children crying

the tambu season lengthening

The Doctor paying to learn

Sandimanite

Suppose a santapee
was to take all Sagomes money
Suppose the creature
from All-play-and-no-work
was to win
a big royalty case
in New York

**Mooma without you**
**I don't where to go**

Suppose flute was to educate heself
and teach you how to blow

**Lord you see how these children behaving**

Suppose fowlcock was to go
to university and so
It don't have so much reason why
he couldn't teach you to crow.

**Mooma without you**
**the breeze lengthening**
**the kaskadura swimming too low**
**You see how the season behaving Lord**
**Papa playing with work in Dorking**
**I don't where to go**
**Cousin fishing for Sagomes money**
**in New York and so**

Santapee santapee

bad black santapee
I blowing me flute and I aaksing you
I educating me cousin sister son
I sandancing
and sweating upsided down
so he can aaks you properly
sans humanity

All the money running
like water gone Venezuela
children lengthening
and the tent-rope crying
forty days and forty nights

     So when the scape-boat rolling upsided down
when the weeds drying
on top the lagoon
and the tent-pole
river-child and sparrow drownding
Float up like a black kaskadura tell the child
Which one-o'-dem you'll be saving

**Mooma**
**without you**
**you see how these children behaving**
**sans humanite**

It had a time
before humming-bird
learn to suck mango
**You can beat that time**
**If you listen to GOOD passeo**

It had a time

cocobay lizard
used to too-loo-loops
all over Latrinite
**If Sparrow say so is so**

It had a time
woman used to horn you
if you couldn't bang pan
or strum cuatro
**When woman say yes**
**They mean me**

It had a time
nice-belly mamma
sell a million roti
to slide all she children
to Panama

**Child**
**make haste**
**come in here and see**
**how your worthless father**
**squinge up he face**
**these forty days**

It had a time
when Urmilia
and all the rest
used to oil their breast
and smooth out their lovely hair
watching their father dhoti
drying out in the air
**If Sparrow say so is so**

Their mother used to say
I call the last one Cynthia
so she wont married no damn Chinee
so she wont go back to India
pose for no light skin people
only wear gold in she nose
when the college boys come out to play
**For when woman say no**
**They mean no**

Child what is your intention
come in out the hot sun
see how your father
strengthening

Sooner than forty year
will bounce up a time
when lizard and santapee
play tambu bamboo
fix their hair
in cane row
first thing in the morning
before humming-bird oil she breast
and Florence fly with me
to look for chinee-mango

when lizard and santapee
play tambu bamboo
fix their hair
in cane row
first thing in the morning
before humming-bird oil she breast
and Florence fly with me

to look for chinee-mango
**You can beat that time**
**If you listen to Good passeo**

So me and you girl
If the season done and the coast is clear
Rest down your basket by the damn lagoon

Flookooks girl come little over here in the bamboo
Dry your nose and soothe out your hair
Come out out they Kaiso tent-hole with some nice ice
Where the population lengthening
Under the mountain crying and your mooma crying
Before you gone to me with your lovely cool drinks

For a pair of college boys only can lime-and rhyme
One way one time a year
Envy you and me Don't know no how
How to raise off their sandimanite coonoo mask

So is me and you girl
And after one hundred and forty year girl
And the mountain crying out this new tambu time girl
And your mother crying for no reason she have to cry

Flookooks

    bring your banja and all your nice cool thing

Over here by me
And let we sing
    And let we do Some stupidness

(London, Easter 1973)

# JUMBIE

I: THE ROAD
II: THE FAMILY
III: WHERE FROM
IV: THE NATURE OF THE LOOK
V: THE LOOK

### I:    The Road

**TOTEM totem**
**name this island**

    **so**

**Yurumi       yulu**
**M'hairo-oun   Mairu**

          **Years ago**
**before sky skyball**
**air**
**before you and you and you**
**Yurumai**

        **Yurumai**

GOODNIGHT cousin friend
Where yo travellin to
with that bigstick
in yo hand
and yo bundle
and yo lantern

It will soon moonlight
**moonlight and lantern**

**mek our marker laugh
from afar**
and you will glad
to travel with me
glad for the companyship
Me and me cuatro can sing good
And I have some rice
and goat meat they leave me
just before the candles wash out

No salt
Salt is for outside people

The moonlight will soon here
But you mean up to now
yo cant tell me goodnight
like a friendly living countryman?

Thanks much   Goodnight again

If you know
how much moon
does fall on this road
sometime
like a big bundle

**What laugh for little children
is bundle for god**

Is where you come out?
Greggs?        I know you
Does oftimes see you
milkin you cow in the mornin
workin like a cattle in the day

comin home late
with you bundle and yo lantern
a bottle of milk for yo children
a bottle of something for yoself
bottlin up yoself for yo wife
I mean to say

You family to those people
on the other side of the island

Every island
have it other side

Before your family move
by Rawacou
from lowside Greggs
they uses to have three cutlass
three whole cattle
a beast
two bucket with handle four children
a yaba coalpot
(you know is which part
your cousin brother and sister are now?)
and a blackanwhite dog
uses was to mek monkey face
every time he see goat
and tear off little girl dress
when they pass by the gate
and chase ground dove and crapaud
and that dog
disappear SO MUCH badmused people
of a nights

I know you well

My name now
is a very old name
is a inside name
from gullyside

        PRANGGA PRANGGA PRANG A
PRANG
      A PRANG PRANG

Yo see this cuatro
You don't **see** this cuatro?

This cuatro here

(Well yo must look
else how I can talk to you
on this lonely road)

This cuatro here now
it have a lot of instruction
from uttermost anciency to the furtherest present time
bout people name
and song
bout is where people come out

It don't must be have a place in the whole world
this cuatro don't know bout

To the other side of this island
it know every moonlight yard
every god village
where moonlight game plays

It make rich people cant sleep

complain
whats laugh and joke for children
is work and big bundle
for mooma and poopa

        I KNOW MOON
            I KNOW STAR
        I WALK THROUGH MOON
                      BETWEEN
STAR
                    I LAY MY
EYEBALL DOWN
                AFAR

WAIT TILL I GET ON THE MOUNTAINTOP
    MY WINGS GOIN TELL YOU
        FILIPPERTYFLOP

Cousin friend I know you
swingin yo lantern goin home
like me every night
swingin yo lantern    like me me cuatro
trying to find where home is

On every side of every island
is a home
is a home
is have to be a home

Greet thou my cuatro
Tell my cuatro goodnight
Say nightnight to me cuatro string

Your children swings

every night
in mama and papa lanternlight

Your children will one day say
flippertyflop
make wings on every mountaintop
under this lonely road

til dog beast cutlass
and moreover mother and father
stop
like a old old name
lay their body down
bundle drop

My rice and goat and music
bellyful of love without salt
say to say goodnight cousin

Cousin goodnight

## II:    The Family

**SAME island**

                                          **same sea**

**air**

        **frame you**
        **frame all island**
                **Yurumai**                **Yulu**

                **frame we**

**AND**   all this time
I mean to say

yo don't even ask me
is where I travellin from

You see that house I just come out of?
nearside the gully by the chicken tree?

**You must look now
Before moonlight rub out everything**

You don't see that house?

Landcrab have house in land
Money have house in hand
But is not there I travellin from

Green live in green
Flood live in river rain in shower
But isnot there I travellin from

**Traveller traveller before moon rain
I will give you a look
a little so
And you will know**

Speak live in song tongue live in drum
Dirt in clean
Life in spirit
Future in mud
Granparents and grandchildren
Live together in a dream

Heart have house in man
Man have house in woman
And we all catchin hell in hell
But that is not the place I travellin from

**You must look now**
**Before moon rub he eye**

Everything in that whole house
is too private
like the people inside it

My outside family

They too private
no inside

Look

>  Poopa with the exercise book
>  writtin down everything he wont able give the fambly
>  next week

Look

>  Alvin with the pignose
>  whale-up with blows for cant learn nothin in school
>  beggin all kind-a God
>  to bring down he girl swellfoot
>  with the prickopay and the winter green
>                                        he only hear bout

Look

>  Mooma and granmooma
>  reading hell out the Bible
>
>  Thirty years ago granpoopa
>                          he dead now
>  has done mark all the sweet chapter
>  with potato peelin

Look

    Titta Clarissa
    feedin she shourteen children zabocca and ferine
    with she right hand
    and ticklin she man trousers
    with she left hand fingernails

Look Cousin
One mornin four o'clock just after slavery
me and another one squeeze een the house. The house
smellin bad. No bread. No pride. Nor any prayer.
We start to cry. The father wake up.
say: **You** can push up yo face like a hundred cemetery.
**Just** show we where
**the** whiteman money bury.

MY DAMMEND OUTER FAMILY

    They don't know me
me and the inside people
who live besides them
who love them and watching over them
straining to help them
from the milk of the chicken tree
the soft of the fowleye
the coconut broom upside down
the hammer and the rule
We the rest of the family
Africa Sion Hill Madeira
Calcutta
Caribisi Gehenna
Mbuntu
Riverbottom
Future moon

**Me Cuatro speak with much instruction**
 **PRANG A PRANG A PRANG PRANG**
**Listen now**
**Before the moonlight oblusterate everything**

 **A PRANG PRANG PRANG**
Me cuatro say
 **THIS HOUSE HAVE ONLY**
  **NOW NOW NOW**
  **NO WHEN**
**NO O N L Y  T H E N**
  **NO HOW NO DAMN HOW**
  **NO NEVER     NO NEVER**
 **NO FOREVER**

For every island have a secret number
For every island have outer people and inner people

Every island have every people
which and while when telling you so
It have good and it have bad jumbie
Likeways good and bad people too

But two bad jumbie don't walk

Signify outer people alone by thyself
is only haffa-people

Signify is the same with we
 is the god same with we

So I travellin WAY from that house
like a lantern swinging
that private house by the gully

where yo cant see it less yo look
and all them half-do people

travellinin a thousand years
a thousand years

I MEAN TO SAY
DOES BIG PEOPLE DON'T SHOULD BUSINESS
IF THEY INSIDE VOICE IS MOST TIME SOUNDS A
LITTLE FUNNY?

. . . But that is not even where I travellin from

### III:     Where From

         now          **FEEL**

                 this island

here
under here

         crabfoot
    asafoetida                  arsifettiti
         duppydirt

air
lovespirit

     fraid

                 (I make from there)

**Underneath everyway**
**Things always makin**
**SOMETHING**     always makin
**Engineer**            **TOTEM**

**Love this island**

                **hear?**

DATTA   damballa
datta ONE
No     Yo rotten-nabel somethin yo
datta NONE

                       **ROUNCE**

Number
no beginning
air     amen
mud    mudwork     place
workwords
up to the isaldn ankle
law
things which binds together
straw    fire    amber
race
root    woodwork

                     atmos

sphere
    Kah-mun
**AND HEREIN ARE THE BEING OF THE FIRST TOTEM**

        Lights
        followin people
        eyes
        of a child lost

                        **JACKLANTERN**

Mothers oversea
blessings
colour on dogs
bell    bucket handle
rainshapes
elbow of a frog
names call behind doors
green
shapes take by smoke

noise inside green things growing up
water
under floors
smell of bones and beads lost
near the joinin of rivers

## HEREIN ARE THE BEING OF THE THIRD TOTEM

Esau Crabfoot
walkin mudstreets
of this island
voice shape like-a hog
bellyful of demon

Maude with her thick socks
In August
day and night

Tomorrow night Sambo Who
will be talkin
to the rat in his shoulder
the whole village people will ring round his place
and sing round his place

Since the time the black bundle
got pull out from their navel
the children of Maude hearty like money
but every mornin
they will spit hungry
and curse the blackan white dog

        **SUCU**        **SUCUAN**
        **JABLISS**    **DIABLESSE**

Four o'clock in the morning
nine mornings before Christmas
children peeping through moon
through the glass of pure rain
crack in the glass
same island
same road
same crossroad
jumbieface
in the glass
of pure rain water

In a river
in Mesopotamia
Arawak rockface
a fancy spoke from afar

Stone fallin on the house of the tief-priest

Navel-strings bury a second time

Christmastime
cramps
linoleum gardens

on rotten floors
crack in the floor

jesuschrist

Strangers

Shoulders bawlin against dangerous winds

Whales
rising up nine times
before death

smells
smiles have to return
nine times after death

## HEREIN ARE THE BEING OF THE NINTH TOTEM

Crossing water
rememberin crossin water
certain children name Maude
fallin teeth
saltin of skins
people walkin away
turnin away
learnin what to not eat

the coming of winds

weapons
fishfields
motherhouses
streets   knowledge   fathers
mothers undersea

under a sea of children
breast    belly
shape like hope

earth open under rope
green doors opening with noise

loudness in trees
blessing what is to eat

the going and coming of winds

Rubbing of eyes
of air
drums

raising from sleep
washing of feet before sleep
sins
spoke with kisses and moaning

blood-drums          bone-flute
death and dancing in one same place

waiting for certain words
the coming and the going of certain words
burdens of knowledge
found at the junction of rivers

## AND HEREIN THUS ARE THE BEING OF THE FORTIETH TOTEM

### IV:    The Nature of the Lock

**BEFORE moon-island**
**raise out the sea**

**I will give you a look**
        **soon so**

    **FORASMUCHAS YOUR INNER NAME**
    **IS A VERY OLD NAME**
Me and my cuatro full of ole time instruction

      **PRANGGA   PRANGGA   PRANG A   PRANG**

Is too much prangga-prang we know
make we have to leave that house
by the gully
It private like hell

Everything I do they wont reconnize me
bring me home

So I have to roam
like some funny old inside name
like a voice without salt
body without no flesh
no family

      **OUTSIDE PEOPLE TODAY**
              **LOUD LIKE MONEY**
    **THEY FOREGET HOW TO DISAPPEAR**
            **HOW TO PROUD**
            **HOW TO PLAY**
  **THEREIN THEY INNER VOICE IS SOUNDING**
              **SOMEHOW FUNNY**
              **SOMEHOW FUNNY**

Traveller traveller
look sometimes what I do
to pleas them back to me

to we
the furtherest people in sleep
among the whole totem of this island

I strettledown the sick child breast
till she laugh out in she sleep
and dance like is cuatro she hear

I plant in one night
jumbie umbrella round the house

one night
I even blow out they candles give them

I MEAN TO SAY
IF I ONCE GIVE THEM A LOOK
DON'T THEY MUST SEE ME?

For children and humble people
have the burden to see
but who will believe them
they is children and humble people

I MEAN TO SAY
I FEEL IT IN MY BONES
ONE DAY SHE I MIGHT FORGET HOW TO APPEAR
THEN WHO WILL LIVEN UP YOUR MOONLIGHT
WHO WILL CARE
WHAT USE IF PEOPLE CANT SEE IN THE NIGHT-
TIME
WHAT THEY CANT SEE IN THE DAY
I MEAN TO SLAY

All of us is cousin
your children is my cousin

my cuatro can make them laugh
Me and you is the same cousin

You know me well
before my family come live by Rawacou
with the blackanwhite puppydog

You and me could meet
many a time
if you have the love
and the fear

After every journey home
each and every moonhead hair will raise
rum will sprinkle on the floor
your woman will curse me
to comfort you
sweep out the house

Six children sound seven goodnight
the oldest broom will sweep
nine cups of milk suffice eight people
and fear will fall you down in your bed

And in your furtherest sleep
your children
will curse youto comfort me

    **LET THE PORTALS AJAR**
**FOR THE TIME IS FAR**
**THE MOTION DEEP**
    **IF YOU WISH TO SEE ME ALLTIME**
        **SAITH OUR MAKER FROM AFAR**
**TAKE HOME ONE OF MY EYES TO KEEP**

**FOR OUR NAME**
**COUSIN**
**IS A VERY OLD NAME**

**A PRANG A PRANG . . .**

**PRANGGGGG**

V: The look

**MOON** rise
**Moon rise**
**Moonrise**
**You ever see**

**EYES**

**LIKE-A THESE?**

DROP your lantern cousin goodnight
and your butu    DONE your long long
burden put all joke aside    END
your bundle of poor children gods bless you

BUT I mean to say
after all this love
twix you
and you and I

YURUMAI    YURUMAI

**Is a big man still business to run**
**inna his own house**
**backwards?**

(5 August - 8 September 1974)

BOOK SIX

# **BROOKLYN THEMES**

September 1982 - February 1983

*For all my friends at the Tiffany's Lounge,
Brooklyn, where all these poems were
conceived and most were written.*

## NOSTRAND AVENUE
*(for Frankie McIntosh)*

The fall is here -- I mean the season -- November,
                                           brother,
In the the new world. Cats locked in hats. Streets are
                                           scented
With garbage. Young dangers roam. Eyeing or buying
This and that, I begin to gather, beforehand, the crisis
Of my winter; for it is here lost in a rented room
I must tackle the first inch of my current future.
I and three other niggers share an ancient shocked
General Electric fridge. We meet not, simply mirror
One another through splintered eyes, food-smells, rigour
And wrench of secret beds, speculated nature of each other's
Garbage, criticisms of November. Yesterday a cripple crossed
My way, inventing his every step. Had he not blocked
The view, I might have discovered (jesus christ) Brooklyn
                                           Bridge!
Sir, I am mesmerised by your greeting, brother.

## JUKE BOX
*(for Hazel)*

I N C O M M U N I C A D O. An altar Tomb. Book with no
                                            name. Noisy
Or stolid as any customer, in fact the nosiest. Yet
                                            of customers
A breed apart. Can any instrument be more arrogant,
                                            more sexless?
Yet you are here to please; and of us according to
                                            his need
May start and re-start your history with a finger and a
                                            quarter,
May penetrate that womb that has no entrance. For
                                            with each act
Of music you tutor us in the mystery of dreams that once
Rocked us solid, of pleasures to come that we hope will
                                            not
Hit us too late. So we worship you, wondering
                                            blasphemously
From our own drunken corner somewhere, how such love
                                            can issue
From a god who cannot dance. Or restless with pain
Who stay so long with you, searching the scriptures.
                                            took you
In shame not to remind ourselves that this nation,
                                            under god,
Has long ago moved on to private computers.
                        Every bar has one.
(Just as every House has a bible somewhere. In a corner.
                        Somewhere.)

# RUTH

Where North Ka' larna abuts on Brooklyn. There stands
Ruth, moody as food, lovely as love down home,
With her child's upper lip. Tough as 52 years,
Tender the way blues intimidate. She owns the stars
That we worship, and all these bottles of liquid passion
Melting like candles under our liquid compassion
For days we all wish to cherish or demolish.
Yet she cannot pronounce the word "business" --
She says "bidness," as if the world,
Bound and bidden,
Had suddenly become a nursery of her enterprise
                                            and her fate.

She will one day help me to restate or
Understand my commitment to jazz. But it seems
Too late to change, too strange a theme to wait for.

And someday, at some pearly portal, at her snowfall,
She will hide her pride behind plates of home-cooked
Longings. Fate and Naomi riding her home.

I am unsure enough of myself

                                to understand that.

## GWEN SINGS

And when Gwen sings her stomach heaves
Like good-natured bread and her hands wink and
the microphone grows hands intercepts her  voice hurls
it at us from somewhere deep inside us
                                       in and yonder
and the sky is blue and so are you and rivers
roll and Rafeek wearing a hat and a piano
and Joel wearing a bass and all the boys roll
and all the sweet dirty things a drum can say
                                         and those
bottles with all their lies eyes that cry bottled up behind
me Ed the trumpeter no hat told me that he hasn't worked
in three weeks and the sun shines bright in my
old stormy weather numbers roll in and out a fat
woman no ribs rolls ass like bread remember tomorrow
haul ass along and VOTE  'cause music music
my love
                       ain't no goddam song

## SONNET FOR MARGARET

Cold, unwashed, often foetal in a bearded bed,
Bald of chest and head, I shall seek
Of all possible endings the mending of love's ache,
And of all deaths the bitter spinal bread
Your youth in me recalls.
Rotund and safe and frightened of our several worlds,
Swaddled in anger and tranquility,
It is a quest not to know what hunger is safe for me,
Nor any longer what is blessing, what is best
For goodness sake.

My dying would be truth if all my youth
Were recalled in you. Lethal, on final ground,
Swaddled in anger and in my bearded bed,
I am by you newly bathed and blest.

## J. SLIGH: A PARABLE

STROLLING one day in mesopotamia, in the valley,
In the dead centre of the garden, the fox
AND his friend the turtle -- an older soldier --
In his shell -- discovered a gru-gru tree.
A gru-gru tree, now, is made of trouble and
Tribulation, covered with thorns and thistles from
Root to top where the tender growing shoot is
Tender and sweet. And sudden so, in a manner
That made all the world's shells quiver, the fox ran up
The tree. And in his ascending his flesh was torn,
And in his descending more blood was born of his
Questionable energy. Amen and hosanna.
James, said the turtle, hardening his shell, Say!
Why did you do that? Because, ventured fox,
                                          eyes radiant,
It seemed a good idea at the time!

But he told no one
        because no one would have understood,
That at the top he had taken into his throat
The shoot, it entering like a flaming sword
That tasted like the truth of the knowledge
Of evil and of good . . .

The turtle, uncomprehending, cast his shell,
                                          grew another,
And has long ago expelled himself from the valley.
Fox walks the garden alone, gardening among shells:
For he cannot, even till this time,
Recall what entered his throat or his mind

That day at the top; or why he had made that
Oh so necessary heartrending climb up the gru-gru,
And down.
Amen and hallelujah, for true

## LOVE IN BED/STUY -- BROOKLYN

Sundays belonged to the Lord
He was the Lord's Anointed

Over a flock of bowed heads
She saw him
Always over a flock of bowed heads
Saw his fingers
Fingering his pulpit his parnassus

Later in the basement
These same fingers would make fried chicken holy

Sunday nights she belonged to him
For this was the way she knew him
The only way
In other basements
After all those frog-nosed hallelujahs
All that finger-lickin' salvation
Only gruff words in a basement
Huffing and healing that promised nothing else
Forever more

Only numberless feelings in the valley of the shadow
In base places in basements
Where dirt and fart and bugs go frolicking
Numberless as the sands on the seashore

Could this be the reason
He disowned her child
The mote in her womb

Because he it was whom God had anointed

Whose fingers smote them all
With healing
Whose unholy anguish made them all holy
In all all the world's basements
Where they came to mourn
And be known

And so that night
All the way to calvary he went for her
And she moaned and shook
Took her place
Her sacred secret sinful place
On the side of Parnassus

And even as he smote her with his healing
She slit his throat

When the real healers came
With their squinting guns their flashing machines
They found her there
The archangel gleaming in her hands

Yes lord they found her there
Still laughing his head off

# THE BAR

THIS bar made a point of being here
The moment I arrived that thirsty Thursday afternoon.
Soon I was to be instructed in its human history:
But it became **this** bar.

                        First you must realise
That bottles match precisely the people
Who come every day to challenge them
                        Scratch, for example,
Bolt upright, liquor up to his shoulders;
And Freckles always wears a red hat. Below,
a freakish yellow. Slow, viscous and dark
                        is Dolores
Like syrup. And the Costa Rican has a voice
Two octaves above his Sunday grin. Pratt, thin
As a pencil; and any time you turn Shotty-Ann
                        around,
You could see clear through to what they have
                        labelled her
On the other side. Southern Comfort goes with
                        Bowlegs and stout.

But with money and with pain, bottles are drained
Daily to the very bottom, and then replaced with
Self-same others on the self-same shelf,
                        no pain at all -- like us --
No pain. Except that out there inside,
                        people are afraid
Of killing one another -- elaborately, cheatingly
                        polite --
How ya doon, honey -- so they kill one another
To test their fear. Where is the honey where the milk?
Here, here honey, the silk and the sack-cloth;
                        just bite --
And lord knows my teeth are no stranger
                        to the flesh of others.

And in here outside, a woman with blood all over
Ran into the store where children were buying
                        rainbow lollipops.

Brewster, intrepid wise-cracker, tall in the saddle,
                        teaches
Drug education in a school. And Ron,
                        patient as a horse,
Talks cars, and his dubious escape from schooling
In the 1930's. D.D. is working at last. Flak

Alas, is sane as hell, and fattening.
                         And in Manhattan
The Supervisor was evil today; and Saul
                    had a stroke,
And Coke is it. And some kids can be crude
Without paying dues, 'cause they clean missed
                        paying dues,
'Cause they never been whipped with a baseball bat
Upside their ass. And Joan hugs her daughter hard
(Messing up her stolen golden earrings) on account of
Her grand-daughter is off recreational drugs.
Behold her. Daddy -- Jesus -- oh shhoot, Daddy,
Where were you?!

Always in the distance a puppy rushes by
In an ambulance, howling like Goliath.
(Shotty-Ann say
       the whole bloody year was an emergency.)

Maybe that is why we use the word
                        "love" so much.

Maybe that is why we purchase so many
                        useless things
With a smile. Maybe that is why

Our greetings are so provocative,
>	seem so rude, so youthful,
>	>	underneath the desperate family love.
Maybe that is why upon occasion
We go to the chinese for food.

The "bathroom" is for "CUSTOMERS ONLY,"
And no selling is allowed.
>	>	Yet for the purchase of a ginger ale
The bathroom is yours. And as for selling,
It is a ritual and a refusal we could not do without.
If you doubt me -- for I am an old defender
Of rituals --
Just imagine some fool youngster came brashing in,
Wearing a wino-colored casket, a bum
Peddling mouthfuls of genuine hand-made heaven.
We would take our time refusing, watching the light
Play on our diminishing bottles. And our Vendor
>	would say,
With retreating spite, meaningless, wise and cool:
>	>	Have a nice day.

# THE ISLANDS (A TOAST)
*(for Arthur Seymour, Guyana)*

St. Vincent, for example,
Blessed little home-home island
Cannot protect its own.

Pigfoot souse is the same everywhere.

Sorrow and strange it is
For a man to have to indicate his roots
With his left hand . . . Goodnight y'all . . .

Manhattan is the richest small island in the world.

There is only one island called Margaret.

There's only two people name Margaret and me
In the whole free world.

In the isle of Brooklyn,
only sturdy shoulders protect me.
Here and there a giggle, a small knife.

My left hand and my right both are withering
Like so many of our tribe.

Pigfoot souse is the same everywhere.

St. Vincent, proud, diminished, giggling, homeless island,
Cannot protect, digest, cannot interpret its own . . .

And yet
Who can ever know the truth
About anything as personal as an island?

EPILOGUE

## ANGEL HORN
*(for Erik)*

When I was born
my father gave to me
an angelhorn
With wings of melody.
That angel placed her lips
upon my finger-tips
and I became, became
her secret name.

Her name grew strong,
Spread like a passion tree.
She named the song,
I played the melody.
And in the morning hour
I awoke to dream of her,
And all day long, day long
I lived her song.

In boat and barge
where songs and seas are friends
our dreams grew large,
made love where dreaming ends.
And people placed her lips
upon our finger-tips,
and friends became, became
our secret name.

Now light is low,
new angels come and go.

The passion tree
Spreads dense as destiny.
And this old angelhorn
strives like the lifting dawn!
Love moves to claim,
to claim our secret name.

(Brooklyn, January 1997)

ABOUT THE AUTHOR

Ellsworth McGranahan "Shake" Keane was born on May 30, 1927, in St. Vincent, Caribbean. Born into a humble family that loved books and music, he completed his early education on the island and worked at the St. Vincent Grammar School as a "pupil-teacher" or teaching assistant of Music, French, and English literature. Taught to play the trumpet by his father, Charles (who died when Keane was thirteen), Keane's first public recital was at age six. At age fourteen, he led a musical band made up of his brothers. In the 1940s, with his mother Dorcas working to raise six children, the teenager joined one of the island's leading bands, Ted Lawrence and His Silvertone Orchestra. The distinctive horn-playing of Keane became a feature of the annual Vincentian carnival, long before he would be called one of the best flugelhorn players in Europe and became known in international jazz circles during the 1950s and 1960s. His complimentary passion to music was poetry, which he had been writing since childhood. (It is still not certain whether the boyhood nickname of "Shake" was short for Shakespeare because Shake so loved literature or for the song *Chocolate Milk Shake* that he loved as a youth.) Before leaving for England in 1952, to study English literature at London University, Keane's first two books, *L'Oubli* (1950, self-published) and *Ixion* (1952) were published. While he did not complete his formal studies in Europe, he recited poetry and prose for and eventually became a producer at *Caribbean Voices*, the influential BBC General Overseas Service program. Keane's commitment to writing was as unabated as the application of his "sharp innovative intelligence" to playing music--mambo, kaiso, highlife, and "free form" jazz. Some of his early poetry, probably because of his music, shows some of the first signs of the jazz inflections that would come to significantly influence Caribbean freestyle and dub poetry decades later. In 1972, the musician who had played with the likes of Lord Kitchener, the Joe Harriot Quintet, and Kurt Edelhagen, was back in the region, reciting his poetry at the first Caribbean Festival of the Arts (CARIFESTA) in Guyana. In 1973, Keane accepted an invitation from the government of St. Vincent to serve as director of culture in Kingstown, capital of the island. In 1975, the department was closed after a change in the colony's government administration. A year later he was appointed principal of Bishop's College in Georgetown, St. Vincent, and taught at the Intermediate High School in the capital. In 1979, St. Vincent, along with eight closely grouped sister islands, emerged from centuries of British colonial rule to become the independent country of St. Vincent and the Grenadines. In that historic year, Keane self-published *The Volcano Suite - A series of five poems*, and he won what is still the most prestigious pan-Caribbean literary prize, Cuba's Premio Casa De Las Americas 1979 Poetry. The winning collection, *One A Week With Water*, was published concurrently in Havana by Casa and remains an essential work of Keane. In 1981, after attending CARIFESTA IV in Barbados, Shake Keane emigrated from his native land to the USA and lived in Brooklyn, New York, with his third wife, Margaret Bynoe. In Brooklyn, he was unable to find immediate work because of his immigrant status and later admitted to feelings of alienation from his "rugged" Bedford-Stuyvesant neighborhood. But the father of three sons, the "musical chameleon," and the poetic iconoclast of "all kinds of 'sacred cows,'" intensified his poetry writing though attended less to his music. His poems have appeared in the literary journals *Bim*, *Kyk-over-al*, *Savacou*, and *Caribbean Quarterly* and have been anthologized in *Caribbean Voices*, *Caribbean Verse*, and *You Better Believe It*. The only CD of his music, *Real Keen: Reggae into Jazz*, was released in 1991 in London. His contemporaries, literary giants, revolutionary poets, scholars, and admirers such as George Lamming, Kamau Brathwaite, Linton Kwesi Johnson, Gordon Rohlehr, Edward Baugh, Adrian Fraser, Philip Nanton, Val Wilmer, and Cecil Blazer Williams are among those who hail Shake Keane as one of the innovative fathers of modern Caribbean literature. *The Angel Horn - Shake Keane (1927-1997) Collected Poems*, an anthology of six unpublished manuscripts, is the fifth[1] and most comprehensive book of Shake Keane's poetic range and vision from the late 1940s to his last poem written in 1997. (The order of the manuscripts and of the poems in each appear in this book as determined by the poet.) At age seventy, ailing with stomach cancer, the gray-bearded giant who towered at six-foot-four, died in Oslo, Norway, in 1997--at the start of a jazz tour. In 2003, Shake Keane, poet, musician, educator, raconteur, "the grand egalitarian," was honored by his country with the unveiling of a life-size bust at the Peace Memorial Hall in Kingstown.

NOTE
[1] Dr. Margaret Bynoe.